Crypto Engine Design

Crypto Engine Design is a deep dive into cryptographic hardware architectures, providing a structured approach to secure computing. This book examines the design, optimization, and implementation of crypto engines, ensuring efficiency and robustness in encryption and hashing mechanisms.

Cryptography is the backbone of digital security, protecting sensitive data from unauthorized access and manipulation. With this book, the goal is to bridge theoretical foundations with practical engineering, making cryptographic systems both accessible and effective. Through a detailed exploration of key algorithms—including **AES**, **DES**, and **SHA**—readers will gain insight into how cryptographic standards operate and how they can be efficiently realized in hardware.

The book unfolds across four chapters:

- **Introduction:** Establishes the fundamental principles of cryptography, highlighting its significance in modern computing.
- **AES:** A deep analysis of the Advanced Encryption Standard, known for its balance between security and performance.
- **DES:** Explores the historical impact and legacy of the Data Encryption Standard, detailing its strengths and limitations.
- **SHA:** Examines Secure Hash Algorithms, emphasizing their role in ensuring data integrity and authenticity.

Designed for professionals, researchers, and engineers, **Crypto Engine Design** serves as both a reference and a practical guide for building high-performance cryptographic hardware solutions. Through clear explanations and structured methodologies, this book equips readers with the tools to implement secure architectures in real-world applications.

Wen-Long Chin is a professor in the Department of Engineering Science at National Cheng Kung University (NCKU), Taiwan, with extensive expertise in cryptographic hardware design and secure computing architectures. Prior to joining academia, He spent over 11 years in the Hsinchu Science Park, Taiwan, specializing in communication and network IC design, where he also led projects in high-performance and secure hardware solutions. As a senior member of IEEE, he contributed to the field through editorial roles, serving as an Associate Editor for *IEEE Wireless Communications*, *IEEE Access*, and the *EURASIP Journal on Wireless Communications and Networking*. His research spans crypto engine optimization, secure circuit implementations, and cryptographic algorithm design, with approximately 70 journal and conference papers, one authored book, entitled *Principles of Verilog Digital Design*, one book chapter, and 17 patents.

Cyber Shorts Series

Discover concise and focused books on specific cybersecurity topics with Cyber Shorts. This book series is designed for students, professionals, and enthusiasts seeking to explore specialized areas within cybersecurity. From blockchain to zero-day to ethical hacking, each book provides real-world examples and practical insights.

Ransomware
Penetration Testing and Contingency Planning
Ravindra Das

Deploying the Zero Trust Framework in MSFT Azure
Ravindra Das

Generative AI
Phishing and Cybersecurity Metrics
Ravindra Das

A Reference Manual for Data Privacy Laws and Cyber Frameworks
Ravindra Das

Offensive and Defensive Cyber Security Strategies
Fundamentals, Theory and Practices
Mariya Ouaissa and Mariyam Ouaissa

Public Key Cryptosystems
Esra Bas

Security Technologies for Law Enforcement Agencies
Kazım Duraklar

Crypto Engine Design
Wen-Long Chin

For more information about this series, please visit: www.routledge.com/Cyber-Shorts/book-series/CYBSH

Crypto Engine Design

Wen-Long Chin

CRC Press
Taylor & Francis Group
Boca Raton London New York

CRC Press is an imprint of the
Taylor & Francis Group, an **informa** business

First edition published 2026
by CRC Press
2385 NW Executive Center Drive, Suite 320, Boca Raton FL 33431

and by CRC Press
4 Park Square, Milton Park, Abingdon, Oxon, OX14 4RN

CRC Press is an imprint of Taylor & Francis Group, LLC

© 2026 Wen-Long Chin

ISBN: 978-1-041-09526-2 (hbk)
ISBN: 978-1-041-09527-9 (pbk)
ISBN: 978-1-003-65055-3 (ebk)

DOI: 10.1201/9781003650553

Typeset in Latin Modern font
by KnowledgeWorks Global Ltd.

Publisher's note: This book has been prepared from camera-ready copy provided by the authors.

Contents

Preface ix

Acknowledgments xi

Chapter 1   Introduction 1
    1.1 Cybersecurity 1
        1.1.1 The Growing Importance of Cybersecurity 1
        1.1.2 Common Cyber Threats 1
        1.1.3 The Role of Technology in Cybersecurity 2
        1.1.4 The Future of Cybersecurity 3
    1.2 Crypto Engine 3
        1.2.1 Crypto Engines Against Cyber Attacks 5
        1.2.2 Challenges in Implementing Crypto Engines 6
        1.2.3 Best Practices for Leveraging Crypto Engines ... 7
    1.3 Data Encryption 9
        1.3.1 Overview of Data Encryption 9
        1.3.2 Traditional Block Ciphers 10
        1.3.3 Challenges and Limitations 11
    1.4 Digital Signature Algorithm 12
        1.4.1 Overview of Digital Signatures 12
        1.4.2 How the Digital Signature Algorithm Works.... 14
        1.4.3 Challenges and Limitations 15

Chapter 2   Advanced Encryption Standard 16
    2.1 AES Encryption Algorithm 17
    2.2 AES Decryption Algorithm 23
    2.3 RTL Designs of Major Processing Steps 26
        2.3.1 Substitute Bytes 27
        2.3.2 Shift Rows 30
        2.3.3 Mix Columns 32
        2.3.4 Add Round Key 36
        2.3.5 Inverse Substitute Bytes 38
        2.3.6 Inverse Shift Rows 40
        2.3.7 Inverse Mix Columns 41
    2.4 Fundamental AES Design 43
    2.5 Unfolded Design 47
    2.6 Sub-pipelined Design 54

2.6.1   AES Encryption 54
2.6.2   AES Decryption..57
2.7   Constructing S-box Using Composite Field
      Arithmetic..58
      2.7.1   Isomorphic Mapping.....................................59
      2.7.2   Multiplicative Inverse over $GF(((2^2)^2)^2)$ 59
      2.7.3   Multiplication over $GF((2^2)^2)$......................60
      2.7.4   Squaring and Multiplication with Constant
              λ over $GF((2^2)^2)$ 62
      2.7.5   Multiplicative Inversion over $GF((2^2)^2)$...........63
      2.7.6   Joint Inverse Isomorphic Mapping and
              Affine Transformation....................................65
2.8   Cipher Block Chaining Mode of Operation..................66
2.9   Post-Quantum Cryptography.....................................70
      2.9.1   Rijndael-256..70

Chapter 3   Data Encryption Standard...72

3.1   Introduction 72
3.2   Initial Permutation..74
3.3   F Block 75
      3.3.1   Expansion 75
      3.3.2   Subkey Mixing..76
      3.3.3   Substitution Box...77
      3.3.4   Permutation..79
3.4   Final Permutation..80
3.5   Subkey Generation 81
      3.5.1   Permuted Choice 1 82
      3.5.2   Rotate...83
      3.5.3   Permuted Choice 2 83
      3.5.4   Final Subkeys 84
3.6   Unfolded and Sub-pipelined Design of DES
      Encryption 87
3.7   Triple DES 89

Chapter 4   Secure Hash Algorithm 90

4.1   Introduction 90
4.2   Message Expansion 92
4.3   Hash Compression...92
4.4   RTL Design..95
4.5   Pipelined SHA-256 Core 99
      4.5.1   Pipelined Compressor 99
      4.5.2   Pipelined Expander 101
4.6   Bitcoin Mining 102

4.7   Bitcoin Mining Architecture 103
        4.7.1   The Architecture in Unfolded Region............. 104
        4.7.2   The Architecture in Iterative Region.............. 105

Index 107

Preface

Cryptography serves as the invisible guardian of digital information, safeguarding our communication, data, and transactions from prying eyes. With Crypto Engine Design, I aim to provide an insightful exploration into the intricacies of cryptographic systems, blending technical depth with practical implementation strategies.

This book is divided into four chapters, each highlighting a cornerstone of modern cryptography. The first chapter, Introduction, sets the stage with foundational concepts, offering readers a clear perspective on the significance and application of cryptography. Subsequent chapters delve into renowned algorithms: Advanced Encryption Standard (AES), which is celebrated for its unmatched security and efficiency; Data Encryption Standard (DES), a pivotal predecessor that shaped the evolution of cryptographic methods; and Secure Hash Algorithm (SHA), which ensures data integrity and authenticity through robust hashing techniques.

Complementing the technical content is the book's cover, a depiction of a serene Chinese ink-wash landscape, embodying the poetic essence of "雲深山靜，孤舟輕蕩，花紅映水，柳絲垂香" — "Cloud-veiled, still hills, Lone boat drifts soft, Red blossoms kiss stream, and Fragrant willows droop." This traditional artistic representation symbolizes the harmony between nature and complexity. Hidden within this artwork, the encrypted ciphertext of these four poetic lines, produced through the AES algorithm, serves as a subtle tribute to the cryptographic theme. The initial key was derived from 20250327 (in ASCII), the date the preface was written, and then hashed using SHA-256 to generate a 256-bit key. Additionally, the poetic words were encoded based on the following codebook. The column and row determine the least and most significant nibbles, respectively. As a result, the plaintext, initial key, ciphertext are 040008890170d10752050c060a0b0383, 07d155a6d656b4eff15093276584bf297d7202d18f917cd8ed61a07d86c801c2, and be3cf1f95648a3ec08be31d24e680ff2, respectively. All are in hexadecimal format. Consequently, the encrypted ciphertext of these four poetic lines is presented as "善溪非念，瓜憂鋼伏，山善霞快，彩狗林玩" on the book's cover, rendering it naturally challenging to decipher.

	00	01	02	03	04	05	06	07	08	09	0a	0b	0c	0d	0e	0f
00	深	孤	石	垂	雲	紅	水	蕩	山	我	柳	絲	映	你	臥	林
10	川	天	地	星	光	日	月	松	竹	梅	菊	春	夏	秋	冬	森
20	海	湖	河	島	峰	壑	谷	崗	塔	陵	台	崖	閣	巒	路	塵
30	雨	霞	雪	霧	晴	晨	暮	夜	波	瀾	流	潺	溪	潮	涌	峽
40	夢	想	情	愛	恨	喜	悲	歡	憂	樂	笑	哭	曉	虹	彩	暗
50	枝	葉	花	樹	草	荷	瓜	桃	李	櫻	杏	梨	柑	榕	桐	他
60	鳥	鷹	雕	燕	鴿	雁	蜜	羊	狗	貓	虎	馬	牛	龍	豬	熊
70	舟	船	廊	門	亭	樓	堡	墻	庭	階	殿	院	堂	廟	碑	鐘
80	清	潔	鮮	香	柔	碎	芳	脆	凝	靜	暖	熱	涼	冷	湛	淡
90	泉	源	浩	湧	潤	泡	港	潭	漢	潟	渡	瀟	滴	滑	渦	泊
a0	金	銀	銅	鋼	鉛	鐵	錫	鋁	琳	玉	琥	璧	瓊	瑰	璋	球
b0	誠	信	義	仁	勇	智	慧	謙	恭	廉	忠	孝	貞	良	善	明
c0	書	畫	詩	文	字	墨	象	紋	跡	謎	言	語	章	記	序	簡
d0	微	輕	快	緩	和	平	穩	靈	活	覺	逐	蠱	守	敏	嚴	恩
e0	飛	跳	行	步	坐	站	躺	躍	飄	翻	落	蹲	伏	踏	蹦	衝
f0	潛	非	玩	舞	歌	吟	唱	聽	看	念	欲	哲	態	聰	慷	慨

It is my hope that this book inspires readers to delve deeper into the realm of cryptographic engine design, merging artistry and precision to build systems that redefine the boundaries of security and innovation.

I am a professor in the Department of Engineering Science at National Cheng Kung University (NCKU), Taiwan, with extensive expertise in cryptographic hardware design and secure computing architectures. Prior to joining academia, I spent over 11 years in the Hsinchu Science Park, Taiwan, specializing in communication and network IC design, where I also led projects in high-performance and secure hardware solutions. As a senior member of IEEE, I have contributed to the field through editorial roles, serving as an Associate Editor for IEEE Wireless Communications, IEEE Access, and the EURASIP Journal on Wireless Communications and Networking. My research spans crypto engine optimization, secure circuit implementations, and cryptographic algorithm design, with approximately 70 journal and conference papers, one authored book, entitled "Principles of Verilog Digital Design", one book chapter, and 17 patents.

Wen-Long Chin

Acknowledgments

This book would not have been possible without the unwavering support of my family. To my wife, Li-Ting, thank you for your endless patience, encouragement, and love—you are the cornerstone of everything I do. To my two sons, Leo and Cheney, your curiosity and boundless energy inspire me every single day. This journey has been enriched by your smiles and laughter, reminding me of the importance of balance and joy in life. This work is as much yours as it is mine. Thank you for being my greatest supporters and my source of strength. I would like to extend my heartfelt gratitude to Gabriella Williams, the Editor at Taylor & Francis Group, as well as the entire Taylor & Francis publishing team for their invaluable support throughout this publication project.

1 Introduction

1.1 CYBERSECURITY

In the modern era, where technology has permeated every aspect of our lives, the importance of cybersecurity cannot be overstated. As the digital landscape expands, so do the threats that target individuals, businesses, and governments. To safeguard the digital world, cybersecurity, the practice of protecting systems, networks, and data from cyber threats, is a crucial aspect of maintaining digital integrity and safety.

Cybersecurity encompasses a broad range of practices, tools, and techniques designed to protect digital assets from unauthorized access, disruption, or destruction. It involves safeguarding information stored on computers, mobile devices, servers, and cloud platforms. The scope of cybersecurity is vast, covering various domains such as network security, application security, information security, and operational security. Each domain addresses specific vulnerabilities and employs tailored strategies to mitigate risks.

1.1.1 THE GROWING IMPORTANCE OF CYBERSECURITY

As the world becomes increasingly interconnected, the reliance on digital technologies grows. From online banking to remote work, people and organizations rely on the Internet for essential activities. This reliance creates opportunities for cybercriminals to exploit vulnerabilities. Cybersecurity is vital to prevent identity theft, financial fraud, and data breaches, which can have devastating consequences for individuals and organizations alike.

For businesses, cybersecurity is not just a technical necessity but also a critical component of reputation management. A single cyberattack can erode customer trust, lead to legal consequences, and result in financial losses. For governments, ensuring cybersecurity is essential for protecting national security, infrastructure, and citizen data.

1.1.2 COMMON CYBER THREATS

Cyber threats are diverse and constantly evolving. Understanding the most common threats is key to implementing effective defense measures.

- Phishing attacks: Cybercriminals use deceptive emails or messages to trick individuals into revealing sensitive information, such as passwords or credit card details.
- Ransomware: Malicious software encrypts a victim's data, demanding a ransom for its release.

DOI: 10.1201/9781003650553-1

- Malware: Various forms of malicious software, such as viruses, worms, and spyware, are designed to disrupt, damage, or gain unauthorized access to systems.
- Denial-of-service (DoS) attacks: Attackers overwhelm a system or network with traffic, rendering it unavailable to users.
- Man-in-the-middle (MitM) attacks: Intercepting communication between two parties to steal data or manipulate information.

1.1.3 THE ROLE OF TECHNOLOGY IN CYBERSECURITY

Technological advancements have significantly enhanced cybersecurity capabilities. Tools such as firewalls, intrusion detection systems, and antivirus software form the first line of defense against cyber threats. Encryption technologies ensure secure communication and data storage. Additionally, digital signature algorithms (DSAs) enable data authenticity, integrity, and non-repudiation. Moreover, artificial intelligence (AI) and machine learning are increasingly used to predict and detect threats by analyzing patterns and anomalies.

Despite these advancements, technology alone cannot guarantee security. Human error remains one of the leading causes of cybersecurity breaches. Therefore, education and awareness play a critical role in enhancing cybersecurity.

To effectively combat cyber threats, individuals and organizations must adopt best practices for cybersecurity. Using strong and unique passwords is a critical first step, as it prevents unauthorized access, especially when combined with multi-factor authentication (MFA), which adds an extra layer of security. Regular software and system updates are vital to patch vulnerabilities and prevent exploitation. Additionally, training and educating users play a pivotal role in reducing risks, as informed users can recognize threats like phishing and handle sensitive data responsibly. Employing antivirus and anti-malware tools, along with firewalls and intrusion detection systems, helps safeguard networks from malicious programs and unauthorized access. Backing up data regularly, following the 3-2-1 rule, ensures critical information can be recovered in case of attacks or disasters. Adopting the principle of least privilege limits access to sensitive data, minimizing the impact of insider threats or compromised accounts. Continuous monitoring and incident response planning are essential for identifying and mitigating risks in real time, supported by security information and event management (SIEM) tools. Securing Internet of things (IoT) devices by changing default credentials, updating firmware, and isolating them on separate networks is increasingly important as IoT adoption grows. Furthermore, organizations must adhere to regulatory standards like general data protection regulation (GDPR) or payment card industry data security standard (PCI DSS) and conduct regular audits to ensure compliance. Finally, implementing a zero-trust architecture, which enforces strict access controls and continuous verification, provides a robust framework for mitigating cyber risks. By integrating these best practices into their cybersecurity strategies, organizations can enhance their resilience and protect their digital assets in an ever-evolving threat landscape.

1.1.4 THE FUTURE OF CYBERSECURITY

As technology evolves, so do the challenges associated with cybersecurity. The rise of the IoT, cloud computing, and 5G networks introduces new vulnerabilities. In the IoT, crypto engines are embedded in devices to enable secure communication, data encryption, and device authentication. They ensure that IoT devices can operate securely in environments with limited resources and high exposure to cyber threats. Cybersecurity must adapt to address these emerging risks. Moreover, the increasing sophistication of cybercriminals necessitates a proactive approach to security.

Collaboration between governments, private organizations, and individuals is critical in the fight against cybercrime. International cooperation is particularly important for addressing threats that transcend borders. Regulations such as the GDPR and initiatives to promote cyber hygiene are steps in the right direction.

Cybersecurity is a dynamic and ever-evolving field that underpins the safety and functionality of the digital world. By understanding the scope of cybersecurity, recognizing common threats, and implementing best practices, individuals and organizations can contribute to a more secure digital environment. As technology continues to advance, a collective commitment to cybersecurity will be essential to safeguarding our interconnected future.

1.2 CRYPTO ENGINE

Cybersecurity, the practice of protecting systems, networks, and data from cyber threats, is a crucial aspect of maintaining digital integrity and safety. Central to this practice is the role of cryptographic engines, commonly referred to as crypto engines, which are integral to ensuring data confidentiality, integrity, and authenticity.

A crypto engine is a specialized hardware or software module designed to perform cryptographic operations. These operations include encryption, decryption, digital signature generation, and verification, as well as hashing. As presented in Figure 1.1, crypto engines are often embedded within devices, systems, or applications to ensure secure communication and data storage. By leveraging advanced mathematical algorithms, crypto engines provide the foundation for secure transactions and data protection in the digital realm.

The synergy between cybersecurity and crypto engines is fundamental to protecting digital systems. Crypto engines serve as the backbone for many cybersecurity measures by enabling secure communication, protecting sensitive data, and verifying the authenticity of users and devices. Their applications

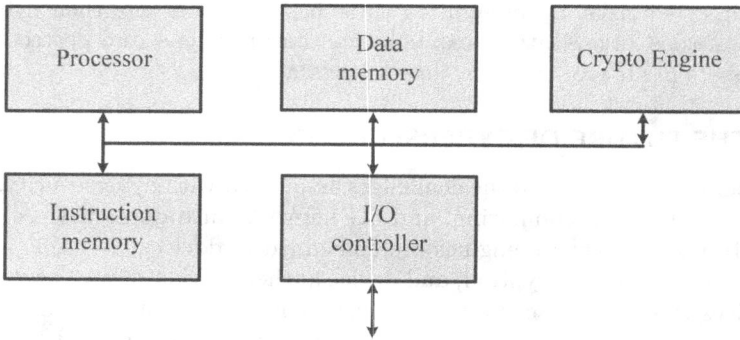

Figure 1.1: Crypto engine in an embedded system, which can be used for a network, storage, or portable device.

include data encryption and decryption, secure communication protocols, digital signatures and authentication, and secure key management.

One of the primary uses of crypto engines is to encrypt sensitive data to ensure its confidentiality using encryption algorithms. By using symmetric or asymmetric encryption algorithms, crypto engines transform plaintext into ciphertext, making the data inaccessible to unauthorized parties. For example, they are used to encrypt data stored on hard drives, transmitted over networks, or processed in the cloud. Decryption, the reverse process, is also handled efficiently by crypto engines, ensuring that only authorized users with the correct keys can access the original data.

Crypto engines are fundamental to the implementation of secure communication protocols such as transport layer security (TLS)/secure sockets layer (SSL), Internet protocol security (IPSec), and hyper text transfer protocol secure (HTTPS). They enable the encryption of data during transmission, preventing eavesdropping and man-in-the-middle attacks. For instance, crypto engines handle the handshake process in SSL/TLS to establish a secure session, generate session keys, and encrypt data exchanged through encrypted channels between parties.

Digital signatures, which provide authentication, integrity, and non-repudiation, rely on cryptographic operations, such as hashing functions, performed by crypto engines. These engines generate and verify digital signatures, ensuring that messages or transactions originate from legitimate sources and remain unaltered by checking the hash value. They are widely used in signing software updates, securing emails, and verifying online identities.

Crypto engines support the secure generation, storage, and distribution of cryptographic keys, which are essential for encryption, decryption, and authentication processes. This includes creating strong keys, securely exchanging them between parties, and managing their lifecycle, such as key rotation and revocation. Proper key management is essential for maintaining the overall security of cryptographic systems.

1.2.1 CRYPTO ENGINES AGAINST CYBER ATTACKS

Crypto engines are powerful tools for countering a wide range of cyberattacks. Below are some of the key types of attacks they mitigate and how they do so:

- Man-in-the-middle (MitM) attacks:
  - How it works: In MitM attacks, an attacker intercepts communication between two parties to steal data or inject malicious content.
  - Crypto engine defense: By using strong encryption protocols like TLS, crypto engines create secure communication channels that prevent attackers from eavesdropping or altering data.
- Phishing attacks:
  - How it works: Attackers trick users into revealing sensitive information by posing as legitimate entities.
  - Crypto engine defense: Crypto engines enable digital signature verification, ensuring the authenticity of websites, emails, and other communications. This helps users identify fraudulent sources.
- Data breaches:
  - How it works: Cybercriminals gain unauthorized access to sensitive data stored in systems or databases.
  - Crypto engine defense: By encrypting data at rest and in transit, crypto engines make stolen data unreadable to unauthorized users.
- Ransomware attacks:
  - How it works: Malware encrypts a victim's data, demanding a ransom for its decryption.
  - Crypto engine defense: Crypto engines facilitate robust backup encryption and integrity checks, ensuring that secure backups remain unaffected by ransomware.
- Replay attacks:
  - How it works: Attackers intercept and retransmit valid data to trick systems into granting unauthorized access.
  - Crypto engine defense: By using unique session keys and time-stamped tokens, crypto engines ensure that communications are valid only within specific contexts.
- Brute-force attacks:
  - How it works: Attackers attempt to crack passwords or encryption keys by systematically trying all possible combinations.
  - Crypto engine defense: Crypto engines implement strong encryption algorithms with sufficiently large key sizes, making brute-force attacks computationally unfeasible.
- Structured query language (SQL) injection:

- How it works: Attackers exploit vulnerabilities in applications to execute malicious SQL queries.
- Crypto engine defense: While not directly mitigating SQL injection, crypto engines protect sensitive data stored in databases through encryption, minimizing the impact of a successful attack.

1.2.2 CHALLENGES IN IMPLEMENTING CRYPTO ENGINES

Implementing crypto engines poses numerous challenges due to the complexity of cryptographic operations and the need to ensure security without compromising performance. One significant challenge is the performance overhead associated with cryptographic processes. Algorithms with large key sizes or intensive operations can introduce latency, particularly in real-time systems or resource-constrained environments like IoT devices. Balancing strong security with efficient performance in these scenarios requires careful optimization.

Another critical issue is effective key management, which involves generating, storing, distributing, and rotating cryptographic keys securely. Any flaws in key management can undermine the security of the entire system, leading to data breaches or unauthorized access. Similarly, ensuring compatibility and seamless integration of crypto engines with various systems, protocols, and standards—such as TLS, IPsec, or FIPS 140-2—can be a complex and time-consuming task. Compatibility gaps often result in delays or security vulnerabilities during implementation.

In resource-limited environments, such as embedded systems and IoT devices, implementing robust cryptographic functionality is particularly challenging. These devices often lack the processing power, memory, or energy required for advanced encryption algorithms, necessitating the development of lightweight crypto engines tailored to their constraints. Additionally, crypto engines, especially hardware implementations, are susceptible to physical attacks and side-channel attacks, such as power analysis or timing attacks. Designing tamper-resistant systems and mitigating such risks increases both the complexity and cost of implementation.

The rapidly evolving landscape of cybersecurity introduces further complications. Staying compliant with updated cryptographic standards, including those addressing emerging threats like quantum computing, requires ongoing updates to crypto engines. Failure to adapt to these changes can leave systems vulnerable to new types of attacks. Moreover, scalability presents challenges in large-scale systems, such as enterprise networks or cloud environments, where managing and synchronizing multiple crypto engines becomes increasingly complex.

Cost is another significant barrier. Developing and deploying secure crypto engines demands specialized expertise, rigorous testing, and substantial resources. This is especially true for hardware-based solutions, such as hardware security modules (HSMs), which can be prohibitively expensive for smaller organizations. Finally, human error during implementation—such as misusing cryptographic libraries or failing to adhere to best practices—can compromise the effectiveness of even the most advanced crypto engines.

In conclusion, while crypto engines are vital for modern cybersecurity, their implementation requires overcoming a range of technical, operational, and financial challenges. Addressing these issues through optimized designs, robust key management, compliance with evolving standards, and careful attention to human factors ensures that crypto engines remain effective in protecting digital systems against an ever-growing array of threats.

1.2.3 BEST PRACTICES FOR LEVERAGING CRYPTO ENGINES

Cybersecurity and crypto engines are inseparable in the mission to safeguard the digital world. As the volume and sophistication of cyber threats increase, crypto engines provide the critical tools needed to protect data, ensure secure communication, and maintain trust in digital systems. By understanding their relationship and adopting advanced cryptographic solutions, individuals and organizations can fortify their defenses against emerging challenges and secure a safer digital future.

Crypto engines are essential components of modern cybersecurity, providing robust cryptographic operations to protect sensitive data and secure communications. To maximize their effectiveness and ensure they are utilized securely and efficiently, organizations and developers must adhere to several best practices.

Selecting the appropriate cryptographic algorithms for your use case is critical. Opt for industry-standard, well-tested algorithms like advanced encryption standard (AES) for symmetric encryption and Rivest-Shamir-Adleman (RSA) or elliptic curve cryptography (ECC) for asymmetric encryption. Ensure that the chosen algorithms meet current security requirements and are resistant to known vulnerabilities. Avoid using outdated or deprecated algorithms like data encryption standard (DES) or MD5 message-digest algorithm.

Robust key management is the cornerstone of secure cryptographic operations. Keys should be generated using high-entropy random number generators, securely stored in hardware modules like HSMs, and rotated periodically. Implement policies for secure key distribution and establish procedures for handling key expiration or compromise. Encrypting keys at rest and in transit further enhances security.

Whenever possible, use hardware-based crypto engines, such as HSMs or trusted platform modules (TPMs), which offer higher performance and better resistance to physical and side-channel attacks. These devices are designed to perform cryptographic operations securely and often come with built-in protections against tampering and unauthorized access. Utilize HSMs, specialized hardware devices, to provide additional layers of security for cryptographic operations. Moreover, dedicated HSMs can offload the workload of central processing unit (CPU) and reduce the overhead of computationally intensive cybersecurity functions. By implementing cryptographic operations in dedicated hardware, crypto engines mitigate risks associated with software-based implementations, such as side-channel attacks and key extraction. Hardware-based crypto engines often include tamper-resistant features to protect keys and sensitive operations from physical attacks.

To mitigate the performance overhead of cryptographic operations, optimize implementations for your specific use case. Use lightweight encryption algorithms for resource-constrained devices, such as IoT sensors. For large-scale applications, leverage hardware acceleration or parallel processing capabilities of modern crypto engines to maintain efficiency.

Keep abreast of evolving cryptographic standards and adopt algorithms and practices recommended by organizations like national institute of standards and technology (NIST) or international organization for standardization (ISO). For example, prepare for the transition to post-quantum cryptography by exploring quantum-resistant algorithms. Regularly update systems to address new vulnerabilities and adhere to compliance requirements like GDPR, HIPAA, or PCI DSS. Conduct thorough testing of crypto engine implementations to ensure they function as intended and meet security requirements. Use cryptographic validation programs, such as cryptographic algorithm validation program (CAVP) of NIST, to verify compliance with standards. Regularly perform vulnerability assessments and penetration testing to identify and address weaknesses.

Restrict access to crypto engines and cryptographic keys to only authorized personnel or applications. Use role-based access controls (RBAC) to minimize exposure. Additionally, implement logging and monitoring mechanisms to detect unauthorized attempts to access or misuse crypto engines.

Ensure that crypto engines are used in conjunction with secure communication protocols, such as TLS/SSL, IPsec, or HTTPS. This ensures data integrity and confidentiality during transmission. Validate the implementation of these protocols to prevent misconfigurations that could weaken security.

Develop an incident response plan for handling cryptographic key compromises or suspected breaches involving crypto engines. This plan should include steps for revoking and replacing keys, reconfiguring systems, and notifying affected parties in compliance with legal and regulatory requirements. Educate developers, administrators, and end-users about the proper use of crypto engines and cryptographic tools. Training reduces the risk of human error, such as misconfigurations or improper handling of cryptographic materials.

The future of cybersecurity will heavily rely on advancements in cryptographic technology. Quantum computing, for instance, poses a significant challenge to current cryptographic methods, as it has the potential to break widely used algorithms. To address this, researchers are developing quantum-resistant cryptographic algorithms that will be implemented in next-generation crypto engines. Moreover, the integration of AI with crypto engines is an emerging trend. AI can enhance cryptographic processes by identifying vulnerabilities, optimizing algorithms, and detecting anomalies in real-time.

1.3 DATA ENCRYPTION

1.3.1 OVERVIEW OF DATA ENCRYPTION

Data encryption is a cornerstone of modern cybersecurity, playing a vital role in protecting sensitive information from unauthorized access, as presented in Figure 1.2. By transforming readable data, known as plaintext, into an unreadable format called ciphertext, encryption ensures that only authorized parties can access the original information. This process relies on cryptographic algorithms and encryption keys to secure data during transmission or storage. By contrast, data decryption is the process of converting encrypted ciphertext back into its original plaintext using the appropriate decryption key or algorithm. Typically, only legal sender and receiver share the same secret key. This mechanism ensures that even if the ciphertext is stolen during transmission through the channel, the stealer still cannot obtain the correct plaintext except users owning the secret key. For the sake of encryption efficiency, the length of plaintext and ciphertext is the same.

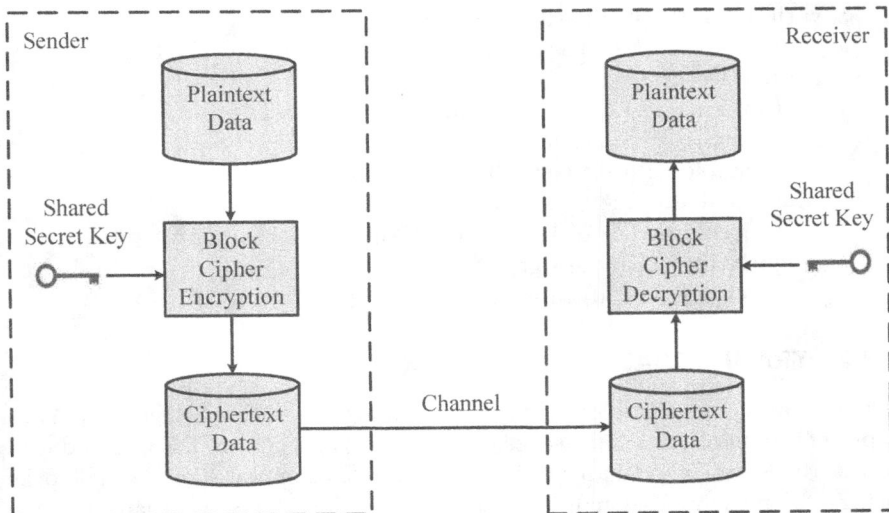

Figure 1.2: Symmetric data encryption and decryption.

Encryption operates through a mathematical algorithm and a key. The algorithm defines the method of transformation, while the key determines how the data is encrypted or decrypted. Without the correct key, deciphering the encrypted data becomes computationally infeasible. Data encryption can be broadly categorized into symmetric and asymmetric encryption. Symmetric encryption uses the same key for both encryption and decryption, making it efficient for encrypting large amounts of data. Examples of symmetric encryption algorithms include the DES, triple DES (3DES), and AES. On the other hand, asymmetric encryption employs a pair of keys: a public key for encryption and a private key for decryption. This method is particularly effective for secure key exchanges and authentication processes. Prominent examples of asymmetric encryption include RSA and ECC. Both approaches form the foundation of modern encryption practices, with their application varying based on specific security requirements and use cases.

Encryption plays an important role in cybersecurity and addresses several key objectives:

- Confidentiality:
  - Ensures that sensitive data remains private, even if intercepted by unauthorized parties.
  - Protects data during transmission (e.g., HTTPS) and storage (e.g., encrypted databases).
  - Examples: DES, 3DES, and AES.
- Integrity:
  - Prevents unauthorized alterations to data by pairing encryption with cryptographic hash functions.
  - Examples: Hash-based message authentication code (HMAC).
- Authentication:
  - Confirms the identity of communicating parties using mechanisms like digital certificates and signatures.
  - Examples: Public key infrastructure (PKI).
- Non-repudiation:
  - Prevents denial of actions by ensuring that a digital signature uniquely identifies the signer.
  - Used in financial transactions and legal agreements.

1.3.2 TRADITIONAL BLOCK CIPHERS

Traditional symmetric block ciphers, including the DES, 3DES, and AES, represent foundational approaches to symmetric encryption. DES, introduced in the 1970s, was a groundbreaking algorithm that operates on 64-bit blocks using a 56-bit key. Although innovative at the time, DES eventually became vulnerable to brute-force attacks due to its relatively short key length. To address these limitations, Triple DES was developed as an enhancement, applying the encryption process three times with either two or three different keys, thereby improving security but at the cost of greater computational intensity. However, even 3DES has been gradually phased out in favor of more robust alternatives. AES, which replaced both DES and 3DES, has become the gold standard in encryption. It processes data in 128-bit blocks and offers key lengths of 128, 192, or 256 bits. AES is renowned for its efficiency and resilience against modern cryptographic attacks, making it widely adopted across various applications, from secure file storage to encrypted online communications.

Data encryption finds applications in a variety of sectors, ensuring secure communication, protecting data during storage, safeguarding financial transactions, and maintaining the confidentiality of healthcare information. For instance, encryption protocols like TLS/SSL are integral to securing internet traffic, websites, emails, and virtual private networks (VPNs), making online communication safe. It also plays a critical role in encrypting files, databases, and backups, thus protecting sensitive information from breaches. The financial industry relies on encryption to secure payment information, adhering to standards like PCI DSS, while the healthcare sector employs encryption to protect electronic health records (EHRs) in compliance with regulations such as health insurance portability and accountability act (HIPAA). By addressing these diverse needs, encryption reinforces trust and security across multiple domains.

1.3.3 CHALLENGES AND LIMITATIONS

Despite its benefits, implementing encryption presents several challenges. Firstly, securely storing, distributing, and rotating cryptographic keys is complex and critical for the key management. Secondly, encryption can add latency, particularly in real-time applications. Therefore, crypto engines implemented using hardware is a popular solution. Thirdly, evolving threats, such as advances in quantum computing, pose a potential risk to current encryption methods. Fourthly, to meet the compliance requirements, organizations must navigate varying regulatory standards for encryption across industries and regions.

As cyber threats continue to evolve, encryption technologies must advance to stay ahead of potential vulnerabilities. The development of quantum-resistant algorithms is one of the primary focuses, as these are designed to withstand the computational power of quantum computers, which could otherwise break traditional encryption methods. Another promising innovation is homomorphic encryption, which allows computations to be performed on encrypted data without requiring decryption, ensuring privacy and security in data processing. Additionally, the integration of AI is expected to optimize encryption processes by identifying vulnerabilities and enhancing algorithm performance. The concept of zero trust architecture further emphasizes the importance of encryption by incorporating it as a core principle to secure access and communication within systems. Together, these advancements represent a proactive approach to maintaining robust encryption in the face of emerging threats.

Data encryption is an indispensable tool in the fight against cyber threats. By securing information at rest and in transit, encryption protects the confidentiality, integrity, and authenticity of digital assets. As technology advances, adopting robust encryption practices and preparing for future challenges will remain critical for individuals, organizations, and governments.

Through continuous innovation and adherence to best practices, encryption will continue to be a cornerstone of cybersecurity in the digital age.

1.4 DIGITAL SIGNATURE ALGORITHM

The DSA is a widely used cryptographic technique designed to ensure the authenticity, integrity, and non-repudiation of digital communications and transactions. It plays a crucial role in various security protocols, helping to safeguard online exchanges, electronic contracts, and software distribution. The development of DSA was driven by the need for a secure and efficient means of verifying the identity of a sender and confirming the integrity of transmitted data without the need for shared secrets.

1.4.1 OVERVIEW OF DIGITAL SIGNATURES

In traditional systems, signatures on paper are used to confirm that a document has been signed by the individual whose name appears on it. These physical signatures are highly trusted because they are difficult to replicate without authorization. In digital systems, the concept of a signature is applied to data, but in a way that protects the message's integrity and authenticity. Digital signatures are based on asymmetric cryptography, which uses a pair of related keys: a private key (held securely by the signer) and a public key (which is distributed widely). Generally, the hash value of the message is the target to be authenticated. Since the length of the hash value is usually much smaller than the original message, the efficiency of the signature (asymmetric encryption) is greatly improved.

The digital signature works by generating a unique hash value (generated by a hash algorithm) of the message, which is then encrypted using the private key, as displayed in Figure 1.3. The encrypted hash is the digital signature, which is sent along with the message. The recipient of the message can decrypt the signature with the sender's public key and compare it to the hash of the message to verify that it has not been altered. This process not only confirms that the message was indeed sent by the holder of the private key but also that the message has remained unmodified during transmission.

The DSA was developed by the national security agency (NSA) in the early 1990s as part of the digital signature standard (DSS) under the U.S. NIST. It was specifically designed to provide a secure and efficient method for generating and verifying digital signatures. The DSA is based on the mathematics of modular exponentiation and the discrete logarithm problem, which is computationally difficult to solve, thereby offering strong security.

The DSA was proposed as a standard in 1994 and was later formalized in the federal information processing standard (FIPS) 186, published by NIST. The DSA is now widely used in various applications such as secure email systems, software distribution, financial transactions, and digital certificates.

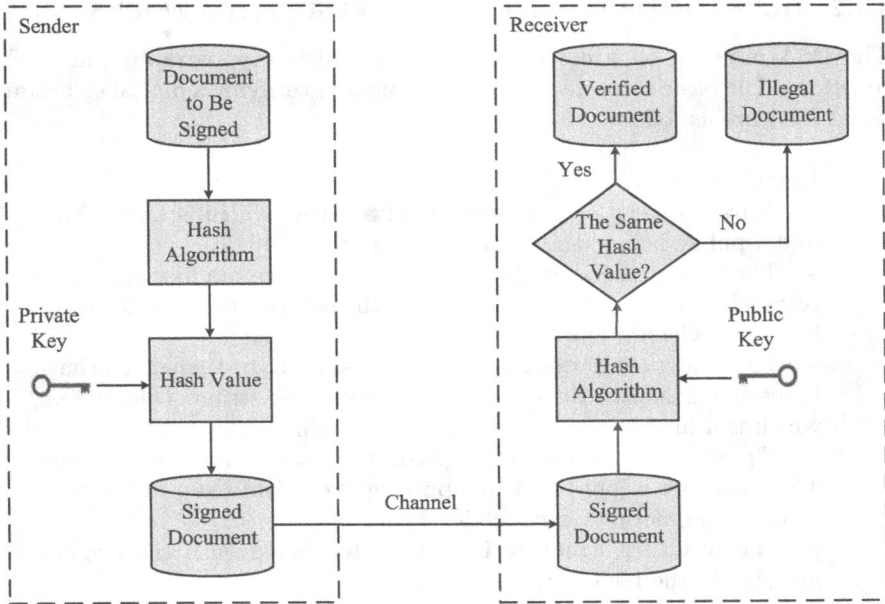

Figure 1.3: Digital signature mechanism.

The applications of DSA are widespread across many fields, owing to its ability to secure digital communications and transactions. In secure communication, DSA is commonly used in email systems to verify the authenticity of messages and protect against phishing and other forms of fraud. By signing emails with a private key, the sender ensures that recipients can trust the message's origin and integrity.

DSA also plays a significant role in software distribution, where it is used to sign software packages, updates, and patches. This ensures that users are downloading genuine software, free from tampering or malware. In the legal and financial sectors, DSA is used to sign contracts, documents, and transactions, providing a secure and verifiable means of electronic signatures that hold legal weight.

Furthermore, DSA, such as secure hash algorithm-256 (SHA-256), is integral to blockchain and cryptocurrency technologies, where it is used in digital wallets to confirm transactions and prevent fraud, maintaining the trustworthiness of the decentralized systems. These diverse applications demonstrate how DSA not only secures communication but also underpins the broader infrastructure of trust in the digital world.

1.4.2 HOW THE DIGITAL SIGNATURE ALGORITHM WORKS

The DSA is based on a combination of public-key cryptography and hash functions. The basic steps involved in creating and verifying a digital signature using DSA are as follows:

- Key Generation:
  - A pair of keys is generated: a private key, which is kept secret, and a public key, which is shared with others.
  - The keys are generated based on a large prime number and a corresponding base value, which ensures the security of the algorithm.
- Signature Generation:
  - The sender computes a hash of the message to be signed. The hash function transforms the message into a fixed-size string of characters, which is a unique representation of the original message.
  - The sender then uses their private key to sign the hash value. The signature is produced by applying the private key to the hash value, using modular arithmetic.
  - The resulting signature is transmitted along with the original message to the recipient.
- Signature Verification:
  - The recipient of the message uses the sender's public key to verify the digital signature.
  - The recipient first computes the hash of the received message and then decrypts the signature using the sender's public key.
  - If the decrypted signature matches the hash value of the received message, the signature is valid, confirming that the message has not been tampered with and that it came from the expected sender.

The DSA offers several key strengths that make it a popular choice in cryptographic systems. One of the primary advantages is its security, as DSA relies on the discrete logarithm problem, which is computationally difficult to solve, providing robust protection against attacks such as brute-force or collision-based methods. The security level of the DSA can be adjusted by increasing the size of the key used, and with sufficiently large keys, the algorithm can offer strong resistance to adversaries.

Additionally, DSA is known for its efficiency. It achieves a high level of security while requiring relatively small key sizes compared to other signature algorithms, like RSA, which helps in speeding up both signing and verification operations. This efficiency is particularly valuable in environments with limited computational resources, such as embedded systems and mobile devices. Another key benefit of DSA is its ability to ensure non-repudiation, meaning that once a message has been signed, the sender cannot deny having signed it. This property is essential in various legal, financial, and contractual contexts where proving the authenticity of a signature is vital.

1.4.3 CHALLENGES AND LIMITATIONS

While the DSA provides strong security and is efficient, it also has some limitations. One key challenge is the management of the private keys. If a private key is compromised, the security of the system is jeopardized. Additionally, DSA requires a secure random number generator for the signing process, and if this randomness is not properly handled, it can lead to vulnerabilities.

Another limitation is that DSA is typically used for signing fixed-size messages (hashes), and it does not provide confidentiality, meaning that the message itself is not encrypted. To address this, DSA is often used in conjunction with other cryptographic techniques, such as encryption algorithms.

The DSA has become a cornerstone of modern cryptographic systems, offering a secure and efficient means of ensuring the authenticity, integrity, and non-repudiation of digital data. Its widespread adoption in various security protocols and applications highlights its importance in safeguarding digital communications and transactions. While it is not without its challenges, the DSA remains a trusted and essential tool in the ongoing effort to secure the digital world.

2 Advanced Encryption Standard

The advanced encryption standard (AES) is widely used in various fields requiring secure and efficient encryption. It is a standard for data protection in government, finance, healthcare, and cloud computing. The AES secures online transactions, wireless communications (Wi-Fi security, VPNs, mobile networks), and secure messaging applications. It is also essential in blockchain technology and cryptographic protocols like TLS/SSL for web security. Additionally, the AES is implemented in embedded systems, IoT devices, and hardware security modules (HSMs) to protect sensitive data. Its high performance and strong security make it a preferred choice in both software and hardware-based encryption solutions.

In addition to introduce the security algorithms for block ciphers, such as AES, this chapter will introduce the design techniques of pipelining and unfolding for them. Moreover, the shared memory architecture that can greatly reduce the required memory space of multiple output queues will also be presented.

In 2001, National Institute of Standard and Technology (NIST) invited proposals for new algorithm of the AES to replace the old data encryption standard (DES). The Rijndael algorithm, designed by two Belgian cryptographers, Joan Daemen and Vincent Rijmen, was finally selected as the AES specification and became a FIPS standard.

Nowadays, AES algorithm is the most popular symmetric block cipher, within which both the outbound and inbound respectively use the same main key for encryption and decryption. Additionally, the AES is an iterative algorithm. The number of iterations is determined by the number of rounds, N_r. There are two additional parameters in the AES algorithm, the number of key, N_k, and the number of blocks, N_b. These three parameters are different in AES-128, AES-192, and AES-256 modes, where the numbers 128, 192, and 256 represent the key lengths in bits. Table 2.1 shows the relationship between these parameters and AES modes.

Table 2.1: The number of keys, N_k, number of blocks, N_b, and number of rounds, N_r, in AES-128, AES-192, and AES-256.

	N_k	N_b	N_r
AES-128	4	4	10
AES-192	6	4	12
AES-256	8	4	14

DOI: 10.1201/9781003650553-2

The block cipher operates on a whole block and requires that the data be padded to a full block if it is smaller than the block size. The 128-bit data block of AES is divided into 16 bytes which are mapped to a 4×4 array. The AES is an iterative algorithm and uses a round function repeatedly. In encryption, each round is composed of four different byte-oriented processing steps: substitute bytes (SubBytes), shift rows (ShiftRows), mix columns (MixColumns), and add round key (AddRoundKey), while the last round does not contain the MixColumns step. In decryption, each round is also composed of four different byte-oriented processing steps: inverse substitute bytes (InvSubBytes), inverse shift rows (InvShiftRows), inverse mix columns (InvMixColumns), and add round key (AddRoundKey), while the last round does not contain the InvMixColumns step.

2.1 AES ENCRYPTION ALGORITHM

The AES is a key-iterative cipher. Rijndael's design philosophy obeys three principles: simplicity, performance, and rationality. Repeatedly using several processing steps makes Rijndael simple. These atomic processing steps can be easily described using operations over the finite field $GF(2^8)$, where $GF(\cdot)$ denotes the Galois field. Besides, simplicity is achieved by maximizing the symmetry in the round function. As such, the decryption simply adopts similar and reverse processing steps of encryption. To receive wide acceptance, Rijndael was designed to achieve high performance and can be efficiently implemented using software or hardware approach on various platforms. For the objective of maintaining the confusion and diffusion in ciphertext, the reasonable structure of Rijndael follows the famous substitution-permutation network (SPN). Rijndael uses substitution based on the multiplicative inverse over the finite field. Its permutation is achieved by the circular shift, and the mixing transformation is borrowed from the theory of error-correcting codes.

AES has a fixed block size of 128 bits for the plaintext, and a key size of 128, 192, or 256 bits. The 128-bit plaintext can be represented by the following two-dimensional (2-D) array,

$$\begin{bmatrix} a_{0,0} & a_{0,1} & a_{0,2} & a_{0,3} \\ a_{1,0} & a_{1,1} & a_{1,2} & a_{1,3} \\ a_{2,0} & a_{2,1} & a_{2,2} & a_{2,3} \\ a_{3,0} & a_{3,1} & a_{3,2} & a_{3,3} \end{bmatrix} \tag{2.1}$$

where $a_{i,j}$ is an 8-bit binary number, called state in AES, $i, j = 0, 1, 2, 3$.

The key size used for an AES cipher indicates the number of rounds that convert the input, i.e., plaintext, into the final output, i.e., ciphertext. The number of rounds is listed below.

- 10 rounds for 128-bit key.
- 12 rounds for 192-bit key.
- 14 rounds for 256-bit key.

The AES encryption algorithm uses multiple rounds to enhance security by ensuring strong confusion and diffusion (Shannon's Principles), making it resistant to cryptanalysis, i.e., the practice of breaking encryption. Each round increases the complexity and randomness of the relationship between the plaintext, ciphertext, and key, preventing attackers from identifying patterns. The avalanche effect ensures that even a small change in input results in a significantly different output, further strengthening encryption. Hence, over successive rounds, a single bit change in plaintext influences many bits in the final ciphertext, which is a characteristic of diffusion. Multiple rounds also defend against attacks, like differential and linear cryptanalysis, while balancing security and performance. With multiple rounds, the AES achieves an optimal trade-off between efficiency and cryptographic strength.

The overall AES encryption algorithm for 128-bit key is displayed in Figure 2.1. Each round consists of a series of operations designed to enhance security and diffusion. The original 128-bit key is expanded into 11 round keys (each 128 bits) by the key expansion function, with one round key used per round, including an initial round key before the first transformation. After 10 rounds, the ciphertext is produced, providing strong encryption security. The decryption process will follow the reverse order with corresponding inverse transformations.

Typically, an encryption algorithm consists of several rounds to maintain the security of a cipher: confusion and diffusion. The confusion principle aims to make the relationship between the ciphertext and the encryption key as complex and unpredictable as possible. By doing so, it ensures that altering a single bit in the key and/or plaintext will cause a drastic change in the resulting ciphertext. This makes it difficult for attackers to deduce the key even if they have multiple pairs of plaintext and ciphertext. Techniques, such as substitution (SubBytes in AES) and XOR operation (AddRoundKey in AES), are commonly used to achieve confusion. Since XOR is a non-reversible operation without the key, this step hides the relationship between plaintext and ciphertext, ensuring that attackers cannot easily derive the key.

Diffusion, on the other hand, aims to spread the influence of each plaintext bit over many ciphertext bits. The goal is to ensure that small changes in the plaintext lead to widespread changes in the ciphertext. This way, statistical patterns in the plaintext are diffused across the ciphertext, making it harder for an attacker to draw conclusions about the plaintext from the ciphertext. Techniques, such as permutation (ShiftRows in AES) and combining (Mix-Columns in AES), are commonly used to achieve confusion.

Together, confusion and diffusion work to make cryptanalysis much more difficult. These principles ensure that encrypted messages are secure and that patterns in the plaintext are well-hidden in the ciphertext.

Specifically, each round of AES consists of several processing steps:

- Initial round key addition: AddRoundKey.

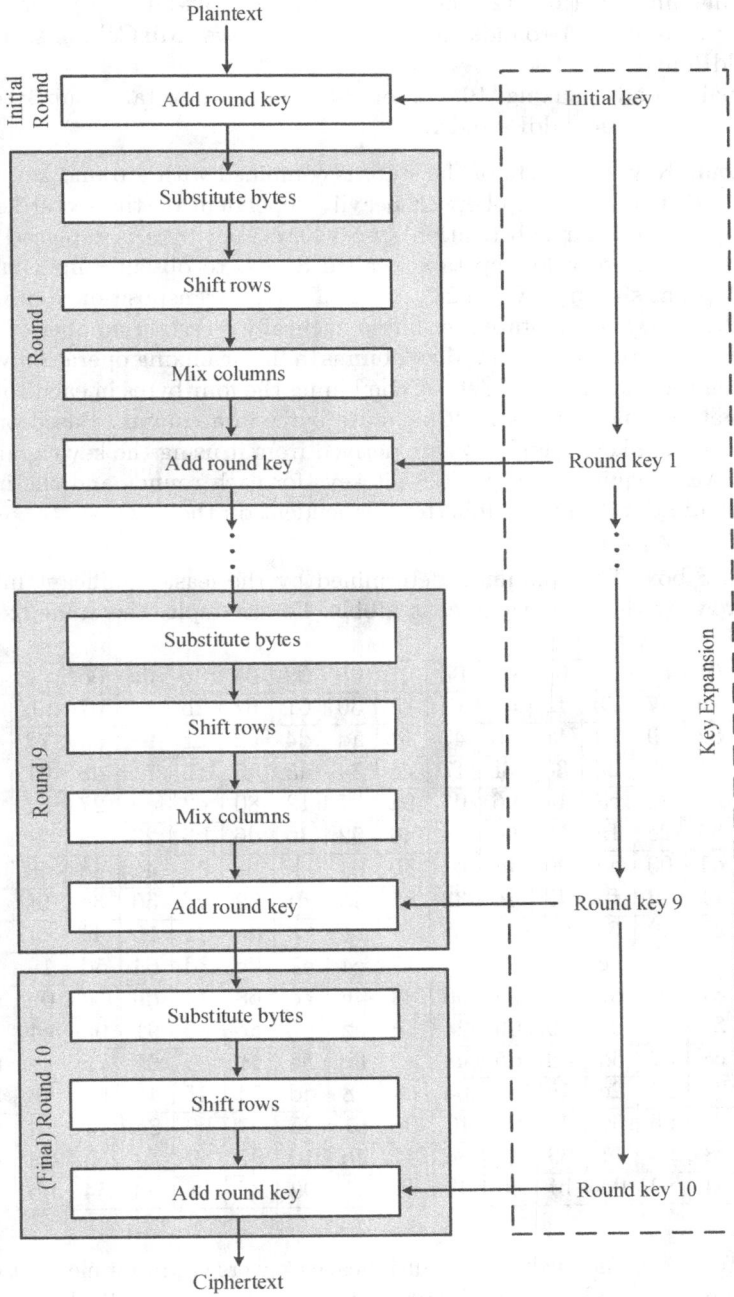

Figure 2.1: Overall AES encryption algorithm of 128-bit key.

- Remaining 9 (for 128-bit key), 11 (for 192-bit key), or 13 (for 256-bit key) rounds: SubBytes, ShiftRows, MixColumns, and AddRoundKey.
- Final round (making 10, 12 or 14 rounds in total): SubBytes, ShiftRows, and AddRoundKey.

In AddRoundKey, each byte of the state is combined with a round key using bitwise XOR, making the ciphertext heavily dependent on the secret key; in SubBytes, a non-linear substitution step where each byte is replaced with another according to a lookup table, called S-box, to obscure input-output relationships, as shown in Table 2.2; in ShiftRows, a transposition step where the last three rows of the state are shifted cyclically a certain number of steps to spread byte dependencies; in MixColumns, a linear mixing operation which operates on the columns of the state, combining the four bytes in each column to propagate changes across multiple state bytes in a column. Based on the initial encryption key, round keys are derived from it using the key expansion function. AES requires multiple 128-bit keys for each rounds and the initial round key addition to make ciphertext dependent on the key.

Table 2.2: S-box. The column is determined by the least significant nibble, and the row by the most significant nibble. For example, the value 0xc7 is converted into 0xc6.

	00	01	02	03	04	05	06	07	08	09	0a	0b	0c	0d	0e	0f
00	63	7c	77	7b	f2	6b	6f	c5	30	01	67	2b	fe	d7	ab	76
10	ca	82	c9	7d	fa	59	47	f0	ad	d4	a2	af	9c	a4	72	c0
20	b7	fd	93	26	36	3f	f7	cc	34	a5	e5	f1	71	d8	31	15
30	04	c7	23	c3	18	96	05	9a	07	12	80	e2	eb	27	b2	75
40	09	83	2c	1a	1b	6e	5a	a0	52	3b	d6	b3	29	e3	2f	84
50	53	d1	00	ed	20	fc	b1	5b	6a	cb	be	39	4a	4c	58	cf
60	d0	ef	aa	fb	43	4d	33	85	45	f9	02	7f	50	3c	9f	a8
70	51	a3	40	8f	92	9d	38	f5	bc	b6	da	21	10	ff	f3	d2
80	cd	0c	13	ec	5f	97	44	17	c4	a7	7e	3d	64	5d	19	73
90	60	81	4f	dc	22	2a	90	88	46	ee	b8	14	de	5e	0b	db
a0	e0	32	3a	0a	49	06	24	5c	c2	d3	ac	62	91	95	e4	79
b0	e7	c8	37	6d	8d	d5	4e	a9	6c	56	f4	ea	65	7a	ae	08
c0	ba	78	25	2e	1c	a6	b4	c6	e8	dd	74	1f	4b	bd	8b	8a
d0	70	3e	b5	66	48	03	f6	0e	61	35	57	b9	86	c1	1d	9e
e0	e1	f8	98	11	69	d9	8e	94	9b	1e	87	e9	ce	55	28	df
f0	8c	a1	89	0d	bf	e6	42	68	41	99	2d	0f	b0	54	bb	16

SubBytes is designed using the multiplicative inverse of input element over $GF(2^8)$, and then applying an affine transformation on the multiplicative inverse. This step is the only non-linear transformation in AES. For the decryption, on the contrary, InvSubBytes is designed applying an inverse affine transformation firstly. The multiplicative inverse over $\mathrm{GF}(2^8)$ of the output of the inverse affine transformation is the final output of the inverse S-box.

Getting rid of the mathematical rigors, in the SubBytes step, each byte $a_{i,j}$ in the state array is substituted with $S(a_{i,j})$ using the 8-bit S-box, as shown in Figure 2.2.

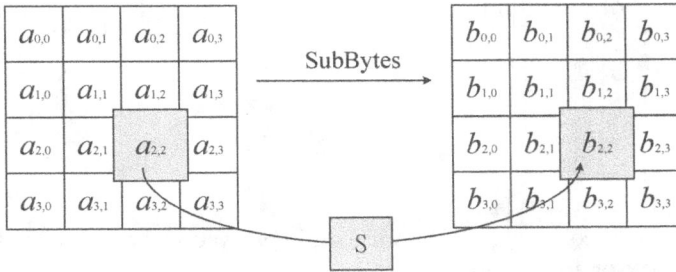

Figure 2.2: The S-box is looked up using $a_{i,j}$.

In the ShiftRows step, the states in each row are cyclically shifted by a certain offset, as shown in Figure 2.3. Specifically, ShiftRows circularly shifts the rows of state array left by its row index.

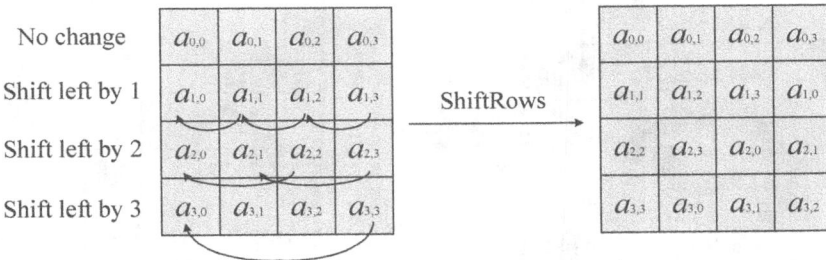

Figure 2.3: States in each row are shifted cyclically to the left. The number of shift differs in each row.

In the MixColumns step, each column is transformed using a fixed matrix (matrix left-multiplied by column gives new value of column in the state), and it can be written as

$$
\begin{bmatrix} b_{0,j} \\ b_{1,j} \\ b_{2,j} \\ b_{3,j} \end{bmatrix} = \begin{bmatrix} 02 & 03 & 01 & 01 \\ 01 & 02 & 03 & 01 \\ 01 & 01 & 02 & 03 \\ 03 & 01 & 01 & 02 \end{bmatrix} \begin{bmatrix} a_{0,j} \\ a_{1,j} \\ a_{2,j} \\ a_{3,j} \end{bmatrix} , j = 0,1,2,3 \tag{2.2}
$$

where $b_{i,j}$ denotes the new state, $i = 0,1,2,3$, and $a_{i,j}$ denotes the old state.

The MixColumns can also be visualized in Figure 2.4.

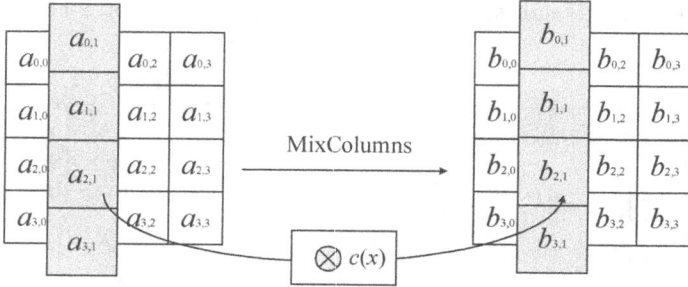

Figure 2.4: Each column of the states can be viewed as being multiplied with a fixed matrix or fixed polynomial, where $c(x)$ denotes the polynomial that linearly combines each column.

In the AddRoundKey step, each byte of the state is added by the corresponding byte of the subkey (or round) using bitwise XOR, as shown in Figure 2.5.

In the AES algorithm, the key expansion function uses the original main key to generate a total of $N_b(N_r+1)$ 4-byte words. Each round key of N_b words

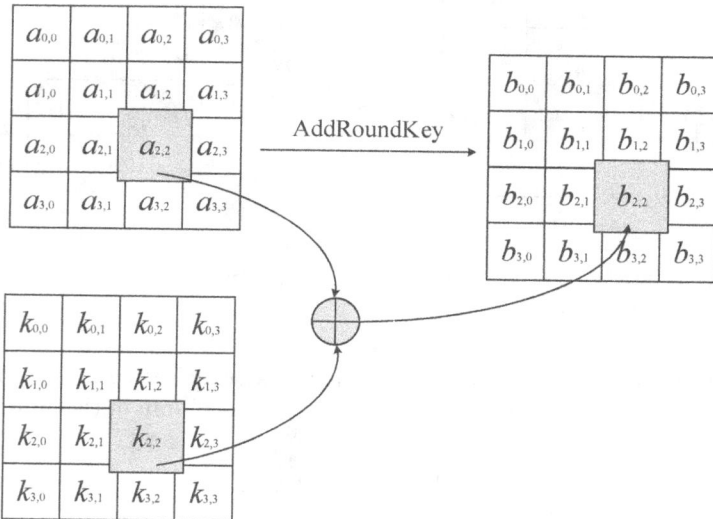

Figure 2.5: Each byte of the state is combined with a byte of the round subkey using the XOR operation.

is used in the AddRoundKey step of a round. The key expansion function is also iterative. The key expansion function can be described by the pseudocode below, where Rcon[·] denotes a 32-bit round constant, RotWord represents a 1-byte left circular shift, and SubWord is an application of the S-box to each of the 4 bytes of the word.

```
KeyExpansion(byte key[4*Nk], word w[Nb*(Nr+1)])
begin
    word temp
    i=0
    while(i<Nk)
        w[i]=word(key[4*i], key[4*i+1], key[4*i+2],
                  key[4*i+3])
        i=i+1
    end while
    i=Nk
    while(i<Nb*(Nr+1))
        temp=w[i-1]
        if(i mod Nk=0)
            temp=SubWord(RotWord(temp)) xor Rcon[i/Nk]
        else if(Nk>6 and i mod Nk=4)
            temp=SubWord(temp)
        end if
        w[i]=w[i-Nk] xor temp
        i=i+1
    end whle
end
```

2.2 AES DECRYPTION ALGORITHM

The AES decryption is computationally efficient and equally secure as encryption, ensuring safe and reliable data recovery when the correct key is provided. The AES decryption follows the principle of reversibility, where each encryption step has a corresponding inverse operation to recover the original plaintext. It relies on inverse transformations, including the inverse S-box for substitution, inverse ShiftRows for row alignment, and inverse MixColumns to reverse diffusion, while AddRoundKey remains unchanged.

The inverse transformations, such as the inverse S-box, inverse ShiftRows, and inverse MixColumns undo their respective encryption transformations. Since the AddRoundKey step remains the same, decryption is only possible with the correct round keys. Hence, the security of decryption is ensured by its strong key dependency, meaning only the correct key can successfully decrypt the ciphertext. Additionally, it systematically reverses the avalanche effect, ensuring that even significant changes in ciphertext (resulted from the strong diffusion on the plaintext) lead back to the correct plaintext without error.

Decryption reconstructs the original plaintext by applying the inverse of each encryption operation in reverse order. As such, the AES decryption algorithm is the inverse process of AES encryption, reversing each transformation step in the same number of rounds (e.g., 10 rounds for a 128-bit key) and the round keys are used in the reverse order.

The AES decryption is a reverse process of AES encryption. The overall AES decryption algorithm for 128-bit key is displayed in Figure 2.6. For 128-bit key (or 10 rounds), by the key expansion function, the encryption key is also expanded into 11 round keys (each 128 bits), which are used in reverse order during decryption. That is, the first round key used in decryption is the last round key used in encryption.

Each round consists of several processing steps:

- Initial round key addition: AddRoundKey.
- Remaining 9 (for 128-bit key), 11 (for 192-bit key), or 13 (for 256-bit key) rounds: InvShiftRows, InvSubBytes, AddRoundKey, and InvMixColumns.
- Final round (making 10, 12, or 14 rounds in total): InvShiftRows, InvSubBytes, and AddRoundKey.

In AddRoundKey of decryption, each byte of the state is combined with the same round key used for encryption using bitwise XOR, eliminating the confusion effect introduced by the secret key; in InvSubBytes, a non-linear substitution step where each byte is replaced with another according to a lookup table, called inverse S-box, as shown in Table 2.3; in InvShiftRows, a transposition step where the last three rows of the state are shifted cyclically a certain number of steps; in InvMixColumns, a linear mixing operation which operates on the columns of the state, combining the four bytes in each column. Based on the initial encryption key, round keys are derived from it using the key expansion function. AES requires multiple 128-bit keys for each round and the initial round key addition.

The InvSubBytes is a reverse function of SubBytes. For example, the value 0xc7 is converted into 0xc6 by the S-box. Then, the value 0xc6 is converted back into 0xc7 by the inverse S-box.

The InvShiftRows is a reverse function of ShiftRows. That is, ShiftRows circularly shifts the rows of state array "left" by its row index. By contrast, InvShiftRows circularly shifts the rows of state array "right" by its row index.

Plaintext

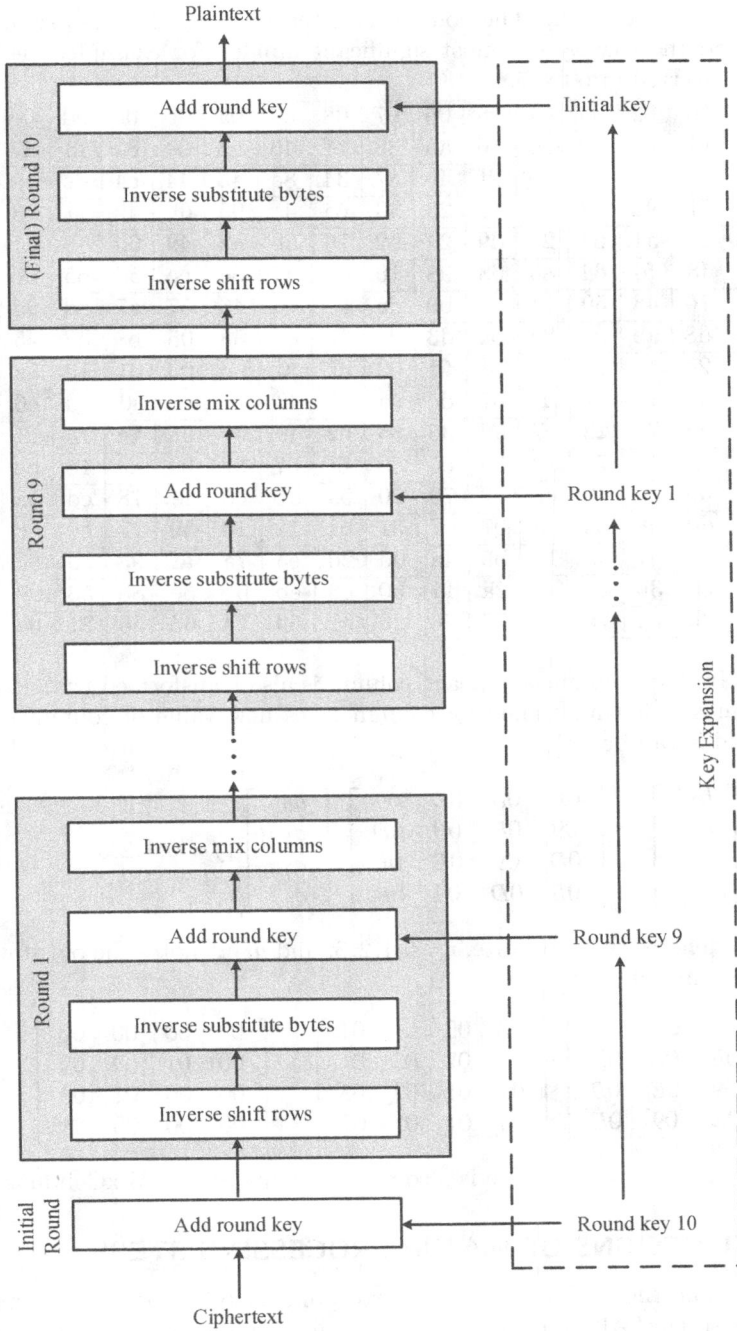

Figure 2.6: Overall AES decryption algorithm of 128-bit key.

Table 2.3: Inverse S-box. The column is determined by the least significant nibble, and the row by the most significant nibble. For example, the value 0xc6 is converted into 0xc7.

	00	01	02	03	04	05	06	07	08	09	0a	0b	0c	0d	0e	0f
00	52	09	6a	d5	30	36	a5	38	bf	40	a3	9e	81	f3	d7	fb
10	7c	e3	39	82	9b	2f	ff	87	34	8e	43	44	c4	de	e9	cb
20	54	7b	94	32	a6	c2	23	3d	ee	4c	95	0b	42	fa	c3	4e
30	08	2e	a1	66	28	d9	24	b2	76	5b	a2	49	6d	8b	d1	25
40	72	f8	f6	64	86	68	98	16	d4	a4	5c	cc	5d	65	b6	92
50	6c	70	48	50	fd	ed	b9	da	5e	15	46	57	a7	8d	9d	84
60	90	d8	ab	00	8c	bc	d3	0a	f7	e4	58	05	b8	b3	45	06
70	d0	2c	1e	8f	ca	3f	0f	02	c1	af	bd	03	01	13	8a	6b
80	3a	91	11	41	4f	67	dc	ea	97	f2	cf	ce	f0	b4	e6	73
90	96	ac	74	22	e7	ad	35	85	e2	f9	37	e8	1c	75	df	6e
a0	47	f1	1a	71	1d	29	c5	89	6f	b7	62	0e	aa	18	be	1b
b0	fc	56	3e	4b	c6	d2	79	20	9a	db	c0	fe	78	cd	5a	f4
c0	1f	dd	a8	33	88	07	c7	31	b1	12	10	59	27	80	ec	5f
d0	60	51	7f	a9	19	b5	4a	0d	2d	e5	7a	af	93	c9	9c	ef
e0	a0	e0	3b	4d	ae	2a	f5	b0	c8	eb	bb	3c	83	53	99	61
f0	17	2b	04	7e	ba	77	d6	26	e1	69	14	63	55	21	0c	7d

In the InvMixColumns step, each column is also transformed using a fixed matrix (matrix left-multiplied by column gives new value of column in the state), and it can be written as

$$
\begin{bmatrix} b_{0,j} \\ b_{1,j} \\ b_{2,j} \\ b_{3,j} \end{bmatrix} = \begin{bmatrix} 0E & 0B & 0D & 09 \\ 09 & 0E & 0B & 0D \\ 0D & 09 & 0E & 0B \\ 0B & 0D & 09 & 0E \end{bmatrix} \begin{bmatrix} a_{0,j} \\ a_{1,j} \\ a_{2,j} \\ a_{3,j} \end{bmatrix}, j = 0, 1, 2, 3 \tag{2.3}
$$

where $b_{i,j}$ denotes the new state, $i = 0, 1, 2, 3$, and $a_{i,j}$ denotes the old state. It can be shown that

$$
\begin{bmatrix} 0E & 0B & 0D & 09 \\ 09 & 0E & 0B & 0D \\ 0D & 09 & 0E & 0B \\ 0B & 0D & 09 & 0E \end{bmatrix} \begin{bmatrix} 02 & 03 & 01 & 01 \\ 01 & 02 & 03 & 01 \\ 01 & 01 & 02 & 03 \\ 03 & 01 & 01 & 02 \end{bmatrix} = \begin{bmatrix} 01 & 00 & 00 & 00 \\ 00 & 01 & 00 & 00 \\ 00 & 00 & 01 & 00 \\ 00 & 00 & 00 & 01 \end{bmatrix}. \tag{2.4}
$$

Therefore, the InvMixColumns is also a reverse function of MixColumns.

2.3 RTL DESIGNS OF MAJOR PROCESSING STEPS

In this section, the RTL designs and corresponding RTL codes of the major processing steps of AES are illustrated in detail. These steps include SubBytes, ShiftRows, and MixColumns for AES encryption; InvSubBytes, InvShiftRows, and InvMixColumns for AES decryption; and AddRoundKey for both AES encryption and decryption.

2.3.1 SUBSTITUTE BYTES

Intuitively, the SubBytes can be implemented using a lookup table, described using a Verilog function as follows. Notably, reusable combinational logics are usually implemented and described using Verilog functions. In the Sbox function below, the inbyte signal and Sbox (function name) are the input and output of the function, respectively. The lookup table is essentially eight sets (or 8 bits) of 256-to-1 multiplexer (for each bit).

```verilog
// S-box implemented using table lookup
function [7:0] Sbox;
  input [7:0] inbyte;
  begin
    case(inbyte)
      8'h00: Sbox=63;8'h01: Sbox=7c;8'h02: Sbox=77;8'h03: Sbox=7b;
      8'h04: Sbox=f2;8'h05: Sbox=6b;8'h06: Sbox=6f;8'h07: Sbox=c5;
      8'h08: Sbox=30;8'h09: Sbox=01;8'h0a: Sbox=67;8'h0b: Sbox=2b;
      8'h0c: Sbox=fe;8'h0d: Sbox=d7;8'h0e: Sbox=ab;8'h0f: Sbox=76;
      8'h10: Sbox=ca;8'h11: Sbox=82;8'h12: Sbox=c9;8'h13: Sbox=7d;
      8'h14: Sbox=fa;8'h15: Sbox=59;8'h16: Sbox=47;8'h17: Sbox=f0;
      8'h18: Sbox=ad;8'h19: Sbox=d4;8'h1a: Sbox=a2;8'h1b: Sbox=af;
      8'h1c: Sbox=9c;8'h1d: Sbox=a4;8'h1e: Sbox=72;8'h1f: Sbox=c0;
      8'h20: Sbox=b7;8'h21: Sbox=fd;8'h22: Sbox=93;8'h23: Sbox=26;
      8'h24: Sbox=36;8'h25: Sbox=3f;8'h26: Sbox=f7;8'h27: Sbox=cc;
      8'h28: Sbox=34;8'h29: Sbox=a5;8'h2a: Sbox=e5;8'h2b: Sbox=f1;
      8'h2c: Sbox=71;8'h2d: Sbox=d8;8'h2e: Sbox=31;8'h2f: Sbox=15;
      8'h30: Sbox=04;8'h31: Sbox=c7;8'h32: Sbox=23;8'h33: Sbox=c3;
      8'h34: Sbox=18;8'h35: Sbox=96;8'h36: Sbox=05;8'h37: Sbox=9a;
      8'h38: Sbox=07;8'h39: Sbox=12;8'h3a: Sbox=80;8'h3b: Sbox=e2;
      8'h3c: Sbox=eb;8'h3d: Sbox=27;8'h3e: Sbox=b2;8'h3f: Sbox=75;
      8'h40: Sbox=09;8'h41: Sbox=83;8'h42: Sbox=2c;8'h43: Sbox=1a;
      8'h44: Sbox=1b;8'h45: Sbox=6e;8'h46: Sbox=5a;8'h47: Sbox=a0;
      8'h48: Sbox=52;8'h49: Sbox=3b;8'h4a: Sbox=d6;8'h4b: Sbox=b3;
      8'h4c: Sbox=29;8'h4d: Sbox=e3;8'h4e: Sbox=2f;8'h4f: Sbox=84;
```

26 8'h50 : Sbox = 53; 8'h51 : Sbox=d1; 8'h52 : Sbox=00; 8'h53 : Sbox=ed ;

27 8'h54 : Sbox = 20; 8'h55 : Sbox=fc ; 8'h56 : Sbox=b1; 8'h57 : Sbox=5b ;

28 8'h58 : Sbox=6a ; 8'h59 : Sbox=cb ; 8'h5a : Sbox=be ; 8'h5b : Sbox=39;

29 8'h5c : Sbox=4a ; 8'h5d : Sbox=4c ; 8'h5e : Sbox = 58; 8'h5f : Sbox=cf ;

30 8'h60 : Sbox=d0 ; 8'h61 : Sbox=ef ; 8'h62 : Sbox=aa ; 8'h63 : Sbox=fb ;

31 8'h64 : Sbox = 43; 8'h65 : Sbox=4d ; 8'h66 : Sbox = 33; 8'h67 : Sbox=85;

32 8'h68 : Sbox = 45; 8'h69 : Sbox=f9 ; 8'h6a : Sbox = 02; 8'h6b : Sbox=7f ;

33 8'h6c : Sbox = 50; 8'h6d : Sbox=3c ; 8'h6e : Sbox=9f ; 8'h6f : Sbox=a8 ;

34 8'h70 : Sbox = 51; 8'h71 : Sbox=a3 ; 8'h72 : Sbox = 40; 8'h73 : Sbox=8f ;

35 8'h74 : Sbox = 92; 8'h75 : Sbox=9d ; 8'h76 : Sbox = 38; 8'h77 : Sbox=f5 ;

36 8'h78 : Sbox=bc ; 8'h79 : Sbox=b6 ; 8'h7a : Sbox=da ; 8'h7b : Sbox = 21;

37 8'h7c : Sbox = 10; 8'h7d : Sbox=ff ; 8'h7e : Sbox=f3 ; 8'h7f : Sbox=d2 ;

38 8'h80 : Sbox=cd ; 8'h81 : Sbox=0c ; 8'h82 : Sbox = 13; 8'h83 : Sbox=ec ;

39 8'h84 : Sbox=5f ; 8'h85 : Sbox = 97; 8'h86 : Sbox = 44; 8'h87 : Sbox=17;

40 8'h88 : Sbox=c4 ; 8'h89 : Sbox=a7 ; 8'h8a : Sbox=7e ; 8'h8b : Sbox=3d ;

41 8'h8c : Sbox = 64; 8'h8d : Sbox=5d ; 8'h8e : Sbox = 19; 8'h8f : Sbox=73;

42 8'h90 : Sbox = 60; 8'h91 : Sbox = 81; 8'h92 : Sbox=4f ; 8'h93 : Sbox=dc ;

43 8'h94 : Sbox = 22; 8'h95 : Sbox=2a ; 8'h96 : Sbox = 90; 8'h97 : Sbox=88;

44 8'h98 : Sbox = 46; 8'h99 : Sbox=ee ; 8'h9a : Sbox=b8 ; 8'h9b : Sbox = 14;

45 8'h9c : Sbox=de ; 8'h9d : Sbox=5e ; 8'h9e : Sbox=0b ; 8'h9f : Sbox=db ;

46 8'ha0 : Sbox=e0 ; 8'ha1 : Sbox = 32; 8'ha2 : Sbox=3a ; 8'ha3 : Sbox=0a ;

47 8'ha4 : Sbox = 49; 8'ha5 : Sbox = 06; 8'ha6 : Sbox = 24; 8'ha7 : Sbox=5c ;

48 8'ha8 : Sbox=c2 ; 8'ha9 : Sbox=d3 ; 8'haa : Sbox=ac ; 8'hab : Sbox = 62;

49 8'hac : Sbox = 91; 8'had : Sbox = 95; 8'hae : Sbox=e4 ; 8'haf : Sbox = 79;

50 8'hb0 : Sbox=e7 ; 8'hb1 : Sbox=c8 ; 8'hb2 : Sbox = 37; 8'hb3 : Sbox=6d ;

51 8'hb4 : Sbox=8d ; 8'hb5 : Sbox=d5 ; 8'hb6 : Sbox=4e ; 8'hb7 : Sbox=a9 ;

52 8'hb8 : Sbox=6c ; 8'hb9 : Sbox = 56; 8'hba : Sbox=f4 ; 8'hbb : Sbox=ea ;

53 8'hbc : Sbox = 65; 8'hbd : Sbox=7a ; 8'hbe : Sbox=ae ; 8'hbf : Sbox=08;

54 8'hc0 : Sbox=ba ; 8'hc1 : Sbox = 78; 8'hc2 : Sbox = 25; 8'hc3 : Sbox=2e ;

55 8'hc4 : Sbox=1c ; 8'hc5 : Sbox=a6 ; 8'hc6 : Sbox=b4 ; 8'hc7 : Sbox=c6 ;

56 8'hc8 : Sbox=e8 ; 8'hc9 : Sbox=dd ; 8'hca : Sbox = 74; 8'hcb : Sbox=1f ;

57 8'hcc : Sbox=4b ; 8'hcd : Sbox=bd ; 8'hce : Sbox=8b ; 8'hcf : Sbox=8a ;

58 8'hd0 : Sbox = 70; 8'hd1 : Sbox=3e ; 8'hd2 : Sbox=b5 ; 8'hd3 : Sbox=66;

59 8'hd4 : Sbox = 48; 8'hd5 : Sbox = 03; 8'hd6 : Sbox=f6 ; 8'hd7 : Sbox=0e ;

60 8'hd8 : Sbox = 61; 8'hd9 : Sbox = 35; 8'hda : Sbox = 57; 8'hdb : Sbox=b9 ;

```
61  8'hdc:Sbox=86;8'hdd:Sbox=c1;8'hde:Sbox=1d;8'hdf:Sbox=9e;
62  8'he0:Sbox=e1;8'he1:Sbox=f8;8'he2:Sbox=98;8'he3:Sbox=11;
63  8'he4:Sbox=69;8'he5:Sbox=d9;8'he6:Sbox=8e;8'he7:Sbox=94;
64  8'he8:Sbox=9b;8'he9:Sbox=1e;8'hea:Sbox=87;8'heb:Sbox=e9;
65  8'hec:Sbox=ce;8'hed:Sbox=55;8'hee:Sbox=28;8'hef:Sbox=df;
66  8'hf0:Sbox=8c;8'hf1:Sbox=a1;8'hf2:Sbox=89;8'hf3:Sbox=0d;
67  8'hf4:Sbox=bf;8'hf5:Sbox=e6;8'hf6:Sbox=42;8'hf7:Sbox=68;
68  8'hf8:Sbox=41;8'hf9:Sbox=99;8'hfa:Sbox=2d;8'hfb:Sbox=0f;
69  8'hfc:Sbox=b0;8'hfd:Sbox=54;8'hfe:Sbox=bb;8'hff:Sbox=16;
70  default:Sbox=63;8'h01:
71  endcase
72  end
73 endfunction
```

To substitute each byte of the input state with a corresponding value from the Sbox, the lookup operation must be performed 16 times in the following RTL codes, where the 16-byte plaintext (or state) is represented (or declared) by 2-D array, sb_inbyte, and the 16-byte output of Sbox is represented by 2-D array, sb_outbyte. The elements of sb_inbyte, i.e., sb_inbyte[0], sb_inbyte[1], sb_inbyte[2], sb_inbyte[3], sb_inbyte[4],..., and sb_inbyte[15] respectively represent $a_{0,0}$, $a_{0,1}$, $a_{0,2}$, $a_{0,3}$, $a_{1,0}$,..., and $a_{3,3}$ in Figure 2.2. Therefore, to repetitively use the Sbox function, the for loop construct can be simply utilized. The for loop in Verilog will be unrolled so that there will be 16 sets of Sbox logic circuits. Notably, the named blocks are utilized to declare the identical local variable, i. Consequently, the SubBytes operation for the 16-byte state is designed to be completed in a single clock cycle.

```
1 wire [7:0] sb_inbyte[0:15];
2 reg [7:0] sb_outbyte[0:15];
3 always @(*) begin: all_Sbox
4    integer i;
5    for(i=0; i<16; i=i+1)
6       sb_outbyte[i]=Sbox(sb_inbyte[i]);
7 end
```

2.3.2 SHIFT ROWS

The ShiftRows is actually a rewiring of the input state array described below. As shown below, the rewiring can be simply described using the continuous assignment, i.e., assign, of Verilog. The 2-D arrays, sr_inbyte and sr_outbyte, are the input and output 4×4 state arrays (in byte), respectively. That is, the elements of sr_inbyte, i.e., sr_inbyte[0], sr_inbyte[1], sr_inbyte[2], sr_inbyte[3], sr_inbyte[4],..., and sr_inbyte[15], respectively represent $a_{0,0}$, $a_{0,1}$, $a_{0,2}$, $a_{0,3}$, $a_{1,0}$,..., and $a_{3,3}$ in Figure 2.3. It can be seen that no logic gates are required. Provided that the fanout load is too large, a logic gate of buffer may be needed.

```verilog
1 // ShiftRows implemented using continuous assignment
2 wire [7:0] sr_inbyte[0:15];
3 wire [7:0] sr_outbyte[0:15];
4 // No change
5 assign {sr_outbyte[0],sr_outbyte[1],sr_outbyte[2],
6         sr_outbyte[3]}={sr_inbyte[0],sr_inbyte[1],
7         sr_inbyte[2],sr_inbyte[3]};
8 // Shift left by 1
9 assign {sr_outbyte[4],sr_outbyte[5],sr_outbyte[6],
10        sr_outbyte[7]}={sr_inbyte[5],sr_inbyte[6],
11        sr_inbyte[7],sr_inbyte[4]};
12 // Shift left by 2
13 assign {sr_outbyte[8],sr_outbyte[9],sr_outbyte[10],
14        sr_outbyte[11]}={sr_inbyte[10],sr_inbyte[11],
15        sr_inbyte[8],sr_inbyte[9]};
16 // Shift left by 3
17 assign {sr_outbyte[12],sr_outbyte[13],sr_outbyte[14],
18        sr_outbyte[15]}={sr_inbyte[15],sr_inbyte[12],
19        sr_inbyte[13],sr_inbyte[14]};
```

Alternatively, the rewiring can also be described using the following Verilog function. Notably, the Verilog function does not support the declaration of 2-D input and output. Therefore, the instate[127:0] is the encapsulated input of 4×4 state arrays (in byte) and the function name ShiftR is the output. Specifically, the elements of instate, i.e., instate[7:0], instate[15:8], instate[23:16], instate[31:24], instate[39:32],..., and instate[127:120], respectively represent $a_{0,0}$, $a_{0,1}$, $a_{0,2}$, $a_{0,3}$, $a_{1,0}$,..., and $a_{3,3}$ in Figure 2.3.

```
 1 // ShiftRows implemented using the function
 2 function [127:0] ShiftR;
 3   input [127:0] instate;
 4   begin
 5   // No change
 6   ShiftR[7:0]=instate[7:0]; ShiftR[15:8]=instate[15:8];
 7   ShiftR[23:16]=instate[23:16]; ShiftR[31:24]=instate[31:24];
 8   // Shift left by 1
 9   ShiftR[39:32]=instate[47:40]; ShiftR[47:40]=instate[55:48];
10   ShiftR[55:48]=instate[63:56]; ShiftR[63:56]=instate[39:32];
11   // Shift left by 2
12   ShiftR[71:64]=instate[87:80]; ShiftR[79:72]=instate[95:88];
13   ShiftR[87:80]=instate[71:64]; ShiftR[95:88]=instate[79:72];
14   // Shift left by 3
15   ShiftR[103:96]=instate[127:120];
16   ShiftR[111:104]=instate[103:96];
17   ShiftR[119:112]=instate[111:104];
18   ShiftR[127:120]=instate[119:112];
19   end
20 endfunction
```

By contrast, to use the ShiftR function, the 2-D input (state), i.e., sr_inbyte, and output (state), i.e., sr_outbyte, should be encapsulated and decapsulated, respectively, as shown below. Notably, the named blocks are utilized to declare the identical local variable, i. Consequently, the ShiftRows operation for the 16-byte state is designed to be completed in a single clock cycle as well.

```
 1 wire [7:0] sr_inbyte[0:15];
 2 reg [7:0] sr_outbyte[0:15];
 3 reg [127:0] sr_instate;
 4 wire [127:0] sr_outstate;
 5 // Change byte array to linear input
 6 always @(*) begin: sr_array_to_linear
 7   integer i;
```

```
 8    for ( i =0; i <16; i=i+1)
 9       sr_instate [(7+8* i ) : 8* i ]=sr_inbyte [ i ];
10 end
11 assign  sr_outstate=ShiftR ( sr_instate );
12 // Change linear output to byte array
13 always  @(*)  begin:  sr_linear_to_array
14    integer  i ;
15    for ( i =0; i <16; i=i+1)
16       sr_outbyte [ i]=sr_outstate [(7+8* i ) : 8* i ];
17 end
```

2.3.3 MIX COLUMNS

The multiplication by the constant matrix in Equation (2.2) for the Mix-Columns can be reduced. For example,

$$
\begin{aligned}
b_{0,j} &= (\{02\} \cdot a_{0,j}) \oplus (\{03\} \cdot a_{1,j}) \oplus a_{2,j} \oplus a_{3,j} \\
&= \text{xtime}(a_{0,j}) \oplus a_{1,j} \oplus \text{xtime}(a_{1,j}) \oplus a_{2,j} \oplus a_{3,j} \\
&= \text{xtime}(a_{0,j} \oplus a_{1,j}) \oplus a_{1,j} \oplus a_{2,j} \oplus a_{3,j}
\end{aligned}
\tag{2.5}
$$

where $\oplus$ denotes the bitwise XOR operation and equals the addition in the Galois field, and $\text{xtime}(a_{i,j}) \equiv \{02\} \cdot a_{i,j}$ and $\{03\} \cdot a_{i,j} = (\{01\} \oplus \{02\}) \cdot a_{i,j} = a_{i,j} \oplus \text{xtime}(a_{i,j})$. Similarly, it can be shown that

$$
\begin{aligned}
b_{1,j} &= a_{0,j} \oplus (\{02\} \cdot a_{1,j}) \oplus (\{03\} \cdot a_{2,j}) \oplus a_{3,j} \\
&= \text{xtime}(a_{1,j} \oplus a_{2,j}) \oplus a_{0,j} \oplus a_{2,j} \oplus a_{3,j},
\end{aligned}
\tag{2.6}
$$

$$
\begin{aligned}
b_{2,j} &= a_{0,j} \oplus a_{1,j} \oplus (\{02\} \cdot a_{2,j}) \oplus (\{03\} \cdot a_{3,j}) \\
&= \text{xtime}(a_{2,j} \oplus a_{3,j}) \oplus a_{0,j} \oplus a_{1,j} \oplus a_{3,j},
\end{aligned}
\tag{2.7}
$$

and

$$
\begin{aligned}
b_{3,j} &= (\{03\} \cdot a_{0,j}) \oplus a_{1,j} \oplus a_{2,j} \oplus (\{02\} \cdot a_{3,j}) \\
&= \text{xtime}(a_{0,j} \oplus a_{3,j}) \oplus a_{0,j} \oplus a_{1,j} \oplus a_{2,j}.
\end{aligned}
\tag{2.8}
$$

The function $\text{xtime}(\cdot)$ is the multiplication by 2 in the Galois field and can be derived by

$$
\text{xtime}(a_{i,j}) = \begin{cases} a_{i,j} \ll 1, & \text{if } a_{i,j}[7] \text{ is 1'b0} \\ (a_{i,j} \ll 1) \oplus \{8\text{'h1b}\}, & \text{if } a_{i,j}[7] \text{ is 1'b1} \end{cases},
\tag{2.9}
$$

where $\ll$ denotes the left shift operation. Notably, the $\text{xtime}(\cdot)$ operation in AES involves multiplying a byte by 2 in the Galois field $GF(2^8)$. This multiplication can be achieved by a left bit-shift. However, when the most significant bit (MSB) of the byte is 1, the result would exceed the 8-bit byte boundary.

To handle this overflow, the result of the left bit-shift needs to be reduced modulo the irreducible polynomial used in AES, which is

$$x^8 + x^4 + x^3 + x + 1. \tag{2.10}$$

This polynomial can be represented as the hexadecimal value 0x11B. Since the MSB is discarded after the shift, we only need to consider the lower 8 bits, represented by 0x1B. So, when the MSB of the byte is 1, the xtime operation includes an additional XOR with 0x1B to correctly reduce the result within the $GF(2^8)$. This ensures that the multiplication stays within the finite field and maintains the desired properties of the AES algorithm.

Before introducing the implementation of MixColumns, we present the hardware implementation of xtime function first. The xtime function is used to multiply an 8-bit input by 2 over $GF(2^8)$ and can be implemented in Figure 2.7, where $\oplus$ denotes the XOR logic gate, $b = $xtime$(a)$, and a and b are 8-bit input and output of the xtime, respectively. Since 8'h1b=8'b00011011 and addition in the Galois field equals the XOR logic, three XOR gates are required.

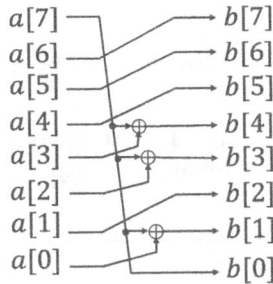

$$
\begin{array}{ll}
a[7] & b[7] \\
a[6] & b[6] \\
a[5] & b[5] \\
a[4] \oplus & b[4] \\
a[3] \oplus & b[3] \\
a[2] & b[2] \\
a[1] \oplus & b[1] \\
a[0] & b[0]
\end{array}
$$

Figure 2.7: Architecture of xtime circuit.

The RTL code of xtime is written below, where inbyte signal and xtime (function name) are 8-bit input and output of the function, respectively.

```
1 // xtime implemented using 3 XOR gates
2 function [7:0] xtime;
3   input [7:0] inbyte;
4   begin
5   xtime={inbyte[6], inbyte[5], inbyte[4],
```

```
6           inbyte[3]^inbyte[7], inbyte[2]^inbyte[7],
7           inbyte[1], inbyte[0]^inbyte[7], inbyte[7]};
8  end
9 endfunction
```

According to Equations (2.5)–(2.8), each column of the new state array of MixColumns can be implemented in Figure 2.8.

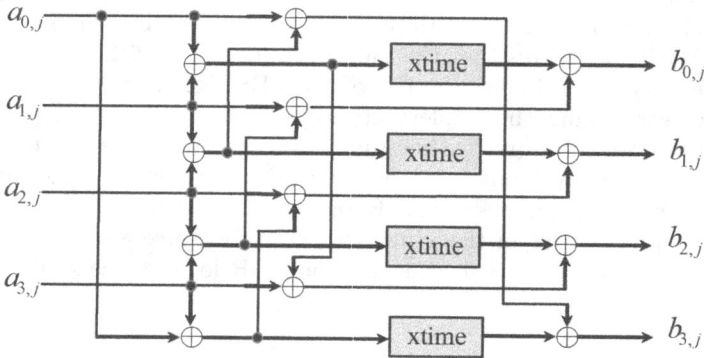

Figure 2.8: Architecture of MixColumns circuit.

The RTL code of MixColumns is written below, where mc_inbyte and mc_outbyte signals are 4-byte input and output columns of state array of MixColumns, respectively.

```
1 // MixColumns implemented using xtime
2 wire [7:0] mc_inbyte[0:3];
3 reg [7:0] mc_outbyte[0:3];
4 always @(*) begin
5   mc_outbyte[0]=xtime(mc_inbyte[0]^mc_inbyte[1])^
6                 mc_inbyte[1]^mc_inbyte[2]^mc_inbyte[3];
7   mc_outbyte[1]=xtime(mc_inbyte[1]^mc_inbyte[2])^
8                 mc_inbyte[0]^mc_inbyte[2]^mc_inbyte[3];
9   mc_outbyte[2]=xtime(mc_inbyte[2]^mc_inbyte[3])^
10                mc_inbyte[0]^mc_inbyte[1]^mc_inbyte[3];
11  mc_outbyte[3]=xtime(mc_inbyte[0]^mc_inbyte[3])^
```

```
12              mc_inbyte[0]^mc_inbyte[1]^mc_inbyte[2];
13 end
```

Alternatively, the MixColumns can also be described using the following Verilog function. Notably, the Verilog function does not support the declaration of 2-D input and output. To this, the 2-D input (state) and output (state) should be decapsulated and encapsulated in Verilog function, respectively.

```
1 // MixColumns implemented using the function
2 function [31:0] MixC;
3   input [31:0] instate;
4   begin
5   MixC[7:0]   =xtime(instate[7:0]^instate[15:8])^
6               instate[15:8]^instate[23:16]^instate[31:24];
7   MixC[15:8]  =xtime(instate[15:8]^instate[23:16])^
8               instate[7:0]^instate[23:16]^instate[31:24];
9   MixC[23:16]=xtime(instate[23:16]^instate[31:24])^
10              instate[7:0]^instate[15:8]^instate[31:24];
11  MixC[31:24]=xtime(instate[7:0]^instate[31:24])^
12              instate[7:0]^instate[15:8]^instate[23:16];
13  end
14 endfunction
```

To use the MixC function, the 2-D input (state), i.e., mc_inbyte, and output (state), i.e., mc_outbyte, should be encapsulated and decapsulated, respectively, as shown below. Please note that the input of MixC function is the column of state instead of row. Hence, please pay attention to the order of encapsulating and decapsulating mc_inbyte and mc_outbyte, respectively. To mix all columns of the input state using the following RTL code, the MixC function must be performed four times. As such, there will be four sets of MixC logic circuits. Consequently, the MixColumns operation for the 16-byte state is also designed to be completed in a single clock cycle.

```
1 wire [7:0]   mc_inbyte[0:15];
2 wire [7:0]   mc_outbyte[0:15];
3 wire [127:0] mc_instate;
```

```
4 reg [127:0] mc_outstate;
5 // Change byte array to linear input
6 assign mc_instate[127:0]=
7   {mc_inbyte[15],mc_inbyte[11],mc_inbyte[7],mc_inbyte[3],
8    mc_inbyte[14],mc_inbyte[10],mc_inbyte[6],mc_inbyte[2],
9    mc_inbyte[13],mc_inbyte[9],mc_inbyte[5],mc_inbyte[1],
10   mc_inbyte[12],mc_inbyte[8],mc_inbyte[4],mc_inbyte[0]};
11 always @(*) begin: all_MixC
12   integer i;
13   for(i=0;i<4;i=i+1)
14     mc_outstate[(31+32*i):32*i]=
15       MixC(mc_instate[(31+32*i):32*i]);
16 end
17 // Change linear output to byte array
18 assign {mc_outbyte[12],mc_outbyte[8],mc_outbyte[4],
19         mc_outbyte[0]}=mc_outstate[31:0];
20 assign {mc_outbyte[13],mc_outbyte[9],mc_outbyte[5],
21         mc_outbyte[1]}=mc_outstate[63:32];
22 assign {mc_outbyte[14],mc_outbyte[10],mc_outbyte[6],
23         mc_outbyte[2]}=mc_outstate[95:64];
24 assign {mc_outbyte[15],mc_outbyte[11],mc_outbyte[7],
25         mc_outbyte[3]}=mc_outstate[127:96];
```

2.3.4 ADD ROUND KEY

The RTL code of AddRoundKey is written below, where ak_keybyte signal is 16-byte subkey (or round key), and ak_inbyte and ak_outbyte signals are 16-byte input and output state arrays of AddRoundKey, respectively.

```
1 // AddRoundKey implemented using XOR gates
2 wire [7:0] ak_inbyte[0:15], ak_keybyte[0:15];
3 reg [7:0] ak_outbyte[0:15];
4 integer i;
5 always @(*)
```

```
6   for ( i =0;  i <16;  i=i +1)
7      ak_outbyte[ i]=ak_inbyte[ i]^ak_keybyte[ i ];
```

Alternatively, the AddRoundKey can also be described using the following Verilog function. Within which, the AddRoundKey operation is performed in one shot, so that 128 XOR logic gates will be inferred.

```
1 // AddRoundKey implemented using the function
2 function [127:0] AddK;
3    input [127:0] instate , keystate;
4    AddK=instate^keystate;
5 endfunction
```

By contrast, to use the AddK function, the 2-D input (state) and output (state) should be encapsulated and decapsulated, respectively, as shown below. Notably, the named blocks are utilized to declare the identical local variable, i.

```
1 wire [7:0] ak_inbyte[0:15];
2 reg [7:0] ak_outbyte[0:15];
3 wire [7:0] ak_keybyte[0:15];
4 reg [127:0] ak_instate;
5 wire [127:0] ak_outstate;
6 reg [127:0] ak_keystate;
7 // Change byte array to linear input
8 always @(*) begin: ak_inarray_to_linear
9    integer i;
10   for ( i =0; i <16; i=i +1)
11      ak_instate[(7+8* i):8* i]=ak_inbyte[ i ];
12 end
13 always @(*) begin: ak_keyarray_to_linear
14   integer i;
15   for ( i =0; i <16; i=i +1)
16      ak_keystate[(7+8* i):8* i]=ak_keybyte[ i ];
17 end
```

```
18 assign ak_outstate=AddK( ak_instate , ak_keystate );
19 // Change linear output to byte array
20 always @(*) begin: ak_linear_to_array
21    integer i ;
22    for ( i =0; i <16; i=i+1)
23       ak_outbyte [ i]=ak_outstate [(7+8* i ) :8* i ];
24 end
```

2.3.5   INVERSE SUBSTITUTE BYTES

The InvSubBytes can also be implemented using a lookup table, described using a Verilog function as follows. The inbyte signal and ISbox (function name) are the input and output of the function, respectively. The lookup table is essentially eight sets (or 8 bits) of 256-to-1 multiplexer (for each bit). Therefore, the inverse S-box has the same architecture as that of S-box.

```
1 // Inverse S–box implemented using table lookup
2 function [7 : 0] ISbox ;
3 input [7 : 0] inbyte ;
4 begin
5 case (inbyte )
6 8 'h00 : ISbox =52;8 'h01 : ISbox =09;8 'h02 : ISbox=6a ;8 'h03 : ISbox=d5 ;
7 8 'h04 : ISbox =30;8 'h05 : ISbox =36;8 'h06 : ISbox=a5 ;8 'h07 : ISbox =38;
8 8 'h08 : ISbox=bf ;8 'h09 : ISbox =40;8 'h0a : ISbox=a3 ;8 'h0b : ISbox=9e ;
9 8 'h0c : ISbox =81;8 'h0d : ISbox=f3 ;8 'h0e : ISbox=d7 ;8 'h0f : ISbox=fb ;
10 8 'h10 : ISbox=7c ;8 'h11 : ISbox=e3 ;8 'h12 : ISbox =39;8 'h13 : ISbox=82;
11 8 'h14 : ISbox=9b ;8 'h15 : ISbox=2f ;8 'h16 : ISbox=ff ;8 'h17 : ISbox=87;
12 8 'h18 : ISbox =34;8 'h19 : ISbox=8e ;8 'h1a : ISbox =43;8 'h1b : ISbox=44;
13 8 'h1c : ISbox=c4 ;8 'h1d : ISbox=de ;8 'h1e : ISbox=e9 ;8 'h1f : ISbox=cb ;
14 8 'h20 : ISbox =54;8 'h21 : ISbox=7b ;8 'h22 : ISbox =94;8 'h23 : ISbox=32;
15 8 'h24 : ISbox=a6 ;8 'h25 : ISbox=c2 ;8 'h26 : ISbox =23;8 'h27 : ISbox=3d ;
16 8 'h28 : ISbox=ee ;8 'h29 : ISbox=4c ;8 'h2a : ISbox =95;8 'h2b : ISbox=0b;
17 8 'h2c : ISbox =42;8 'h2d : ISbox=fa ;8 'h2e : ISbox=c3 ;8 'h2f : ISbox=4e ;
18 8 'h30 : ISbox =08;8 'h31 : ISbox=2e ;8 'h32 : ISbox=a1 ;8 'h33 : ISbox=66;
19 8 'h34 : ISbox =28;8 'h35 : ISbox=d9 ;8 'h36 : ISbox =24;8 'h37 : ISbox=b2 ;
20 8 'h38 : ISbox =76;8 'h39 : ISbox=5b ;8 'h3a : ISbox=a2 ;8 'h3b : ISbox=49;
```

21 8 'h3c : ISbox=6d ; 8 'h3d : ISbox=8b ; 8 'h3e : ISbox=d1 ; 8 'h3f : ISbox=25;

22 8 'h40 : ISbox = 72;8 'h41 : ISbox=f8 ; 8 'h42 : ISbox=f6 ; 8 'h43 : ISbox=64;

23 8 'h44 : ISbox=86;8 'h45 : ISbox = 68;8 'h46 : ISbox = 98;8 'h47 : ISbox=16;

24 8 'h48 : ISbox=d4 ; 8 'h49 : ISbox=a4 ; 8 'h4a : ISbox=5c ; 8 'h4b : ISbox=cc ;

25 8 'h4c : ISbox=5d ; 8 'h4d : ISbox = 65;8 'h4e : ISbox=b6 ; 8 'h4f : ISbox=92;

26 8 'h50 : ISbox=6c ; 8 'h51 : ISbox = 70;8 'h52 : ISbox = 48;8 'h53 : ISbox=50;

27 8 'h54 : ISbox=fd ; 8 'h55 : ISbox=ed ; 8 'h56 : ISbox=b9 ; 8 'h57 : ISbox=da ;

28 8 'h58 : ISbox=5e ; 8 'h59 : ISbox = 15;8 'h5a : ISbox = 46;8 'h5b : ISbox=57;

29 8 'h5c : ISbox=a7 ; 8 'h5d : ISbox=8d ; 8 'h5e : ISbox=9d ; 8 'h5f : ISbox=84;

30 8 'h60 : ISbox = 90;8 'h61 : ISbox=d8 ; 8 'h62 : ISbox=ab ; 8 'h63 : ISbox=00;

31 8 'h64 : ISbox=8c ; 8 'h65 : ISbox=bc ; 8 'h66 : ISbox=d3 ; 8 'h67 : ISbox=0a ;

32 8 'h68 : ISbox=f7 ; 8 'h69 : ISbox=e4 ; 8 'h6a : ISbox = 58;8 'h6b : ISbox=05;

33 8 'h6c : ISbox=b8 ; 8 'h6d : ISbox=b3 ; 8 'h6e : ISbox = 45;8 'h6f : ISbox=06;

34 8 'h70 : ISbox=d0 ; 8 'h71 : ISbox=2c ; 8 'h72 : ISbox=1e ; 8 'h73 : ISbox=8f ;

35 8 'h74 : ISbox=ca ; 8 'h75 : ISbox=3f ; 8 'h76 : ISbox=0f ; 8 'h77 : ISbox = 02;

36 8 'h78 : ISbox=c1 ; 8 'h79 : ISbox=af ; 8 'h7a : ISbox=bd ; 8 'h7b : ISbox=03;

37 8 'h7c : ISbox = 01;8 'h7d : ISbox = 13;8 'h7e : ISbox=8a ; 8 'h7f : ISbox=6b ;

38 8 'h80 : ISbox=3a ; 8 'h81 : ISbox = 91;8 'h82 : ISbox = 11;8 'h83 : ISbox=41;

39 8 'h84 : ISbox=4f ; 8 'h85 : ISbox = 67;8 'h86 : ISbox=dc ; 8 'h87 : ISbox=ea ;

40 8 'h88 : ISbox = 97;8 'h89 : ISbox=f2 ; 8 'h8a : ISbox=cf ; 8 'h8b : ISbox=ce ;

41 8 'h8c : ISbox=f0 ; 8 'h8d : ISbox=b4 ; 8 'h8e : ISbox=e6 ; 8 'h8f : ISbox=73;

42 8 'h90 : ISbox = 96;8 'h91 : ISbox=ac ; 8 'h92 : ISbox = 74;8 'h93 : ISbox = 22;

43 8 'h94 : ISbox=e7 ; 8 'h95 : ISbox=ad ; 8 'h96 : ISbox = 35;8 'h97 : ISbox=85;

44 8 'h98 : ISbox=e2 ; 8 'h99 : ISbox=f9 ; 8 'h9a : ISbox = 37;8 'h9b : ISbox=e8 ;

45 8 'h9c : ISbox=1c ; 8 'h9d : ISbox = 75;8 'h9e : ISbox=df ; 8 'h9f : ISbox=6e ;

46 8 'ha0 : ISbox = 47;8 'ha1 : ISbox=f1 ; 8 'ha2 : ISbox=1a ; 8 'ha3 : ISbox = 71;

47 8 'ha4 : ISbox=1d ; 8 'ha5 : ISbox = 29;8 'ha6 : ISbox=c5 ; 8 'ha7 : ISbox=89;

48 8 'ha8 : ISbox=6f ; 8 'ha9 : ISbox=b7 ; 8 'haa : ISbox = 62;8 'hab : ISbox=0e ;

49 8 'hac : ISbox=aa ; 8 'had : ISbox = 18;8 'hae : ISbox=be ; 8 'haf : ISbox=1b ;

50 8 'hb0 : ISbox=fc ; 8 'hb1 : ISbox = 56;8 'hb2 : ISbox=3e ; 8 'hb3 : ISbox=4b ;

51 8 'hb4 : ISbox=c6 ; 8 'hb5 : ISbox=d2 ; 8 'hb6 : ISbox = 79;8 'hb7 : ISbox=20;

52 8 'hb8 : ISbox=9a ; 8 'hb9 : ISbox=db ; 8 'hba : ISbox=c0 ; 8 'hbb : ISbox=fe ;

53 8 'hbc : ISbox = 78;8 'hbd : ISbox=cd ; 8 'hbe : ISbox=5a ; 8 'hbf : ISbox=f4 ;

54 8 'hc0 : ISbox=1f ; 8 'hc1 : ISbox=dd ; 8 'hc2 : ISbox=a8 ; 8 'hc3 : ISbox=33;

55 8 'hc4 : ISbox = 88;8 'hc5 : ISbox = 07;8 'hc6 : ISbox=c7 ; 8 'hc7 : ISbox=31;

```
56 8 'hc8 : ISbox=b1 ; 8 'hc9 : ISbox =12;8 'hca : ISbox =10;8 'hcb : ISbox =59;
57 8 'hcc : ISbox =27;8 'hcd : ISbox =80;8 'hce : ISbox=ec ;8 'hcf : ISbox=5f ;
58 8 'hd0 : ISbox =60;8 'hd1 : ISbox =51;8 'hd2 : ISbox=7f ;8 'hd3 : ISbox=a9 ;
59 8 'hd4 : ISbox =19;8 'hd5 : ISbox=b5 ;8 'hd6 : ISbox=4a ;8 'hd7 : ISbox=0d ;
60 8 'hd8 : ISbox=2d ;8 'hd9 : ISbox=e5 ;8 'hda : ISbox=7a ;8 'hdb : ISbox=af ;
61 8 'hdc : ISbox =93;8 'hdd : ISbox=c9 ;8 'hde : ISbox=9c ;8 'hdf : ISbox=ef ;
62 8 'he0 : ISbox=a0 ;8 'he1 : ISbox=e0 ;8 'he2 : ISbox=3b ;8 'he3 : ISbox=4d ;
63 8 'he4 : ISbox=ae ;8 'he5 : ISbox=2a ;8 'he6 : ISbox=f5 ;8 'he7 : ISbox=b0 ;
64 8 'he8 : ISbox=c8 ;8 'he9 : ISbox=eb ;8 'hea : ISbox=bb ;8 'heb : ISbox=3c ;
65 8 'hec : ISbox =83;8 'hed : ISbox =53;8 'hee : ISbox =99;8 'hef : ISbox =61;
66 8 'hf0 : ISbox =17;8 'hf1 : ISbox=2b ;8 'hf2 : ISbox =04;8 'hf3 : ISbox=7e ;
67 8 'hf4 : ISbox=ba ;8 'hf5 : ISbox =77;8 'hf6 : ISbox=d6 ;8 'hf7 : ISbox =26;
68 8 'hf8 : ISbox=e1 ;8 'hf9 : ISbox =69;8 'hfa : ISbox =14;8 'hfb : ISbox =63;
69 8 'hfc : ISbox =55;8 'hfd : ISbox =21;8 'hfe : ISbox=0c ;8 'hff : ISbox=7d ;
70 default : ISbox =52;
71 endcase
72 end
73 endfunction
```

2.3.6 INVERSE SHIFT ROWS

The InvShiftRows is actually a rewiring of the input state array described below. The rewiring can be simply described using the following Verilog function. Notably, the Verilog function does not support the declaration of 2-D input and output. Therefore, the instate[127:0] is the encapsulated input of 4×4 state arrays (in byte) and the function name IShiftR is the output. It can be seen that no logic gates are required. Provided that the fanout load is too large, a logic gate of buffer may be needed.

```
1 // InvShiftRows implemented using the function
2 function [127 : 0] IShiftR ;
3 input [127 : 0] instate ;
4 begin
5 // No change
6 IShiftR [7 :0]= instate [7 : 0]; IShiftR [15 : 8]= instate [15 : 8];
7 IShiftR [23 : 16]= instate [23 : 16]; IShiftR [31 : 24]= instate [31 : 24];
```

```
 8// Shift right by 1
 9 IShiftR [39 : 32]=instate [63 : 56]; IShiftR [47 : 40]=instate [39 : 32];
10 IShiftR [55 : 48]=instate [47 : 40]; IShiftR [63 : 56]=instate [55 : 48];
11// Shift right by 2
12 IShiftR [71 : 64]=instate [87 : 80]; IShiftR [79 : 72]=instate [95 : 88];
13 IShiftR [87 : 80]=instate [71 : 64]; IShiftR [95 : 88]=instate [79 : 72];
14// Shift right by 3
15 IShiftR [103 : 96]=instate [111 : 104];
16 IShiftR [111 : 104]=instate [119 : 112];
17 IShiftR [119 : 112]=instate [127 : 120];
18 IShiftR [127 : 120]=instate [103 : 96];
19 end
20 endfunction
```

2.3.7 INVERSE MIX COLUMNS

The multiplication by constant matrix in Equation (2.3) for the InvMix-Columns can be separated and rewritten as

$$
\begin{bmatrix} b_{0,j} \\ b_{1,j} \\ b_{2,j} \\ b_{3,j} \end{bmatrix} = \begin{bmatrix} b'_{0,j} \\ b'_{1,j} \\ b'_{2,j} \\ b'_{3,j} \end{bmatrix} + \begin{bmatrix} b''_{0,j} \\ b''_{1,j} \\ b''_{2,j} \\ b''_{3,j} \end{bmatrix} + \begin{bmatrix} b'''_{0,j} \\ b'''_{1,j} \\ b'''_{2,j} \\ b'''_{3,j} \end{bmatrix}, \tag{2.11}
$$

where

$$
\begin{bmatrix} b'_{0,j} \\ b'_{1,j} \\ b'_{2,j} \\ b'_{3,j} \end{bmatrix} = \begin{bmatrix} 02 & 03 & 01 & 01 \\ 01 & 02 & 03 & 01 \\ 01 & 01 & 02 & 03 \\ 03 & 01 & 01 & 02 \end{bmatrix} \begin{bmatrix} a_{0,j} \\ a_{1,j} \\ a_{2,j} \\ a_{3,j} \end{bmatrix}, \tag{2.12}
$$

$$
\begin{bmatrix} b''_{0,j} \\ b''_{1,j} \\ b''_{2,j} \\ b''_{3,j} \end{bmatrix} = \begin{bmatrix} 08 & 08 & 08 & 08 \\ 08 & 08 & 08 & 08 \\ 08 & 08 & 08 & 08 \\ 08 & 08 & 08 & 08 \end{bmatrix} \begin{bmatrix} a_{0,j} \\ a_{1,j} \\ a_{2,j} \\ a_{3,j} \end{bmatrix}, \tag{2.13}
$$

and

$$
\begin{bmatrix} b'''_{0,j} \\ b'''_{1,j} \\ b'''_{2,j} \\ b'''_{3,j} \end{bmatrix} = \begin{bmatrix} 04 & 00 & 04 & 00 \\ 00 & 04 & 00 & 04 \\ 04 & 00 & 04 & 00 \\ 00 & 04 & 00 & 04 \end{bmatrix} \begin{bmatrix} a_{0,j} \\ a_{1,j} \\ a_{2,j} \\ a_{3,j} \end{bmatrix}. \tag{2.14}
$$

Notice that the multiplications of Equations (2.12) and (2.2) are the same. Therefore, the same circuit in Figure 2.8 can be used to obtain $b'_{0,j}$, $b'_{1,j}$, $b'_{2,j}$, and $b'_{3,j}$.

Next, according to Equation (2.13), it can be observed that

$$b''_{0,j} = b''_{1,j} = b''_{2,j} = b''_{3,j}, \tag{2.15}$$

and

$$\begin{aligned} b''_{0,j} &= 8 \times a_{0,j} + 8 \times a_{1,j} + 8 \times a_{2,j} + 8 \times a_{3,j} \\ &= \text{xtime}\left(\text{xtime}\left(\text{xtime}\left(a_{0,j} + a_{1,j} + a_{2,j} + a_{3,j}\right)\right)\right). \end{aligned} \tag{2.16}$$

Moreover, based on Equation (2.14), one has

$$b'''_{0,j} = b'''_{2,j} = \text{xtime}\left(\text{xtime}\left(a_{0,j} + a_{2,j}\right)\right), \tag{2.17}$$

and

$$b'''_{1,j} = b'''_{3,j} = \text{xtime}\left(\text{xtime}\left(a_{1,j} + a_{3,j}\right)\right). \tag{2.18}$$

According to Equations (2.11)–(2.18), each column of the new state array of InvMixColumns can be implemented in Figure 2.9.

The RTL code of InvMixColumns is written below. Notably, the Verilog function does not support the declaration of 2-D input and output. To this, the 2-D input (state) and output (state) should be decapsulated and encapsulated in Verilog function, respectively. Therefore, the instate[31:0] is the

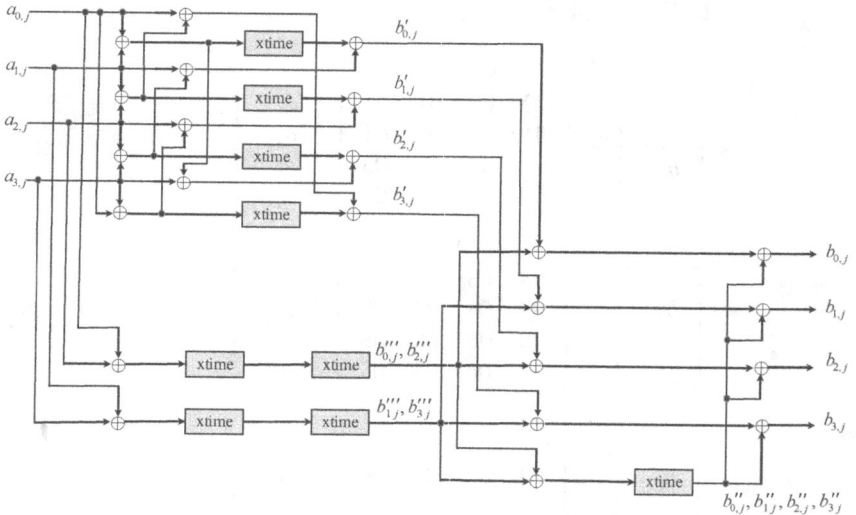

Figure 2.9: Architecture of InvMixColumns circuit.

encapsulated input of 4-byte column of state array and the function name
InvMixC is the output. To mix four columns of 4×4 state array, there will
be four sets of InvMixC logic circuits.

```
1 // InvMixColumns implemented using the function
2 function [31:0] InvMixC;
3   input [31:0] instate;
4   reg [31:0] prime1, prime2, prime3;
5   begin
6   prime1[7:0]=xtime(instate[7:0]^instate[15:8])^
7                 instate[15:8]^instate[23:16]^instate[31:24];
8   prime1[15:8]=xtime(instate[15:8]^instate[23:16])^
9                 instate[7:0]^instate[23:16]^instate[31:24];
10  prime1[23:16]=xtime(instate[23:16]^instate[3])^
11                 instate[7:0]^instate[15:8]^instate[31:24];
12  prime1[31:24]=xtime(instate[7:0]^instate[31:24])^
13                 instate[7:0]^instate[15:8]^instate[23:16];
14  prime3[7:0]=xtime(xtime(instate[7:0]^instate[23:16]));
15  prime3[23:16]=prime3[7:0];
16  prime3[15:8]=xtime(xtime(instate[15:8]^instate[31:24]));
17  prime3[31:24]=prime3[15:8];
18  prime2[7:0]=xtime(prime3[7:0]^prime3[15:8]);
19  prime2[15:8]=prime2[7:0];
20  prime2[23:16]=prime2[7:0];
21  prime2[31:24]=prime2[7:0];
22  InvMixC[7:0]=prime1[7:0]^prime3[7:0]^prime2[7:0];
23  InvMixC[15:8]=prime1[15:8]^prime3[15:8]^prime2[15:8];
24  InvMixC[23:16]=prime1[23:16]^prime3[23:16]^prime2[23:16];
25  InvMixC[31:24]=prime1[31:24]^prime3[31:24]^prime2[31:24];
26  end
27 endfunction
```

2.4 FUNDAMENTAL AES DESIGN

After introducing the RTL designs of the major processing steps of AES, this
section presents the fundamental AES design optimized for minimal area. In
this design, all rounds of AES are folded to conserve circuit area, as presented

Plaintext

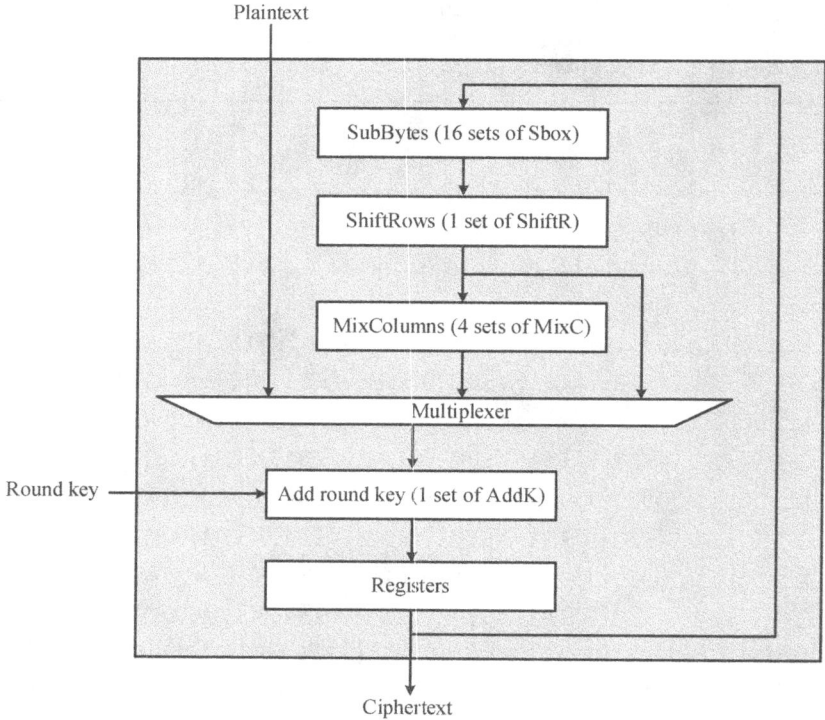

Figure 2.10: Folded AES single-round one-cycle design.

in Figure 2.10. The area complexity is approximately equivalent to that of a single round, with each round being completed in a single cycle. This is why it is termed a single-round one-cycle design. As a result, all major processing steps in AES encryption are reused and instantiated only once, with pipeline registers added to avoid combinational loops. Multiplexers choose between three inputs—plaintext, output of ShiftRows, and output of MixColumns—for the AddRoundKey operation, based on the round counter (not depicted in the figure).

Specifically, for the initial round, only the AddRoundKey operation is needed. Consequently, the multiplexers select the plaintext, which is then XORed with the round key (the initial key for the first round). The resulting output is stored in registers for the subsequent round. For the remaining nine rounds (for a 128-bit key), the operations SubBytes, ShiftRows, MixColumns, and AddRoundKey are performed in sequence. As a result, the multiplexers select the output of MixColumns to serve as the input for the AddRoundKey operation. In the final round, only the SubBytes, ShiftRows, and AddRoundKey operations are executed in sequence. Thus, the multiplexers select the output of ShiftRows as the input for the AddRoundKey operation. Following the final round, the output stored in the register is the ciphertext.

The RTL codes for the folded AES encryption design, as illustrated in Figure 2.10, are detailed below. The AES encryption module leverages previously defined functions of major processing steps. It's important to note that while 2-D array declarations are allowed in data type declarations, they are not permitted for port declarations. The control unit operates primarily based on the round counter (rnd_cnt), the input valid (in_valid), and the output valid (out_valid) signals. Given that the output valid signal clearly indicates the availability of the output ciphertext, there's no need to reset the pipeline register, ctstate, which helps in saving circuit area.

```
1 // Folded single—round AES encryption implemented using
2 // a module
3 module FoldAESEnc(out_valid, ctstate, in_valid, ptstate,
4                   keystate, clk, rst_n);
5 output out_valid;
6 output [127:0] ctstate;
7 input in_valid;
8 input [127:0] ptstate, keystate;
9 input clk, rst_n;
10 reg [3:0] rnd_cnt; // round counter
11 reg out_valid;
12 reg [127:0] ctstate;
13 reg [127:0] sb_outstate, mc_outstate, mux_outstate;
14 wire [127:0] sr_outstate, ak_outstate;
15 parameter FINAL_CNT=10;
16 // Round counter to generate control signals
17 always @(posedge clk or negedge rst_n)
18        if(!rst_n)
19            rnd_cnt<=0;
20    else if(rnd_cnt==FINAL_CNT)
21            rnd_cnt<=0;
22    else if(in_valid || rnd_cnt!=FINAL_CNT)
23            rnd_cnt<=rnd_cnt+1;
24 // SubBytes operation
```

```verilog
25 always @(*) begin: AESEnc_Sbox
26   integer i;
27   for(i=0; i<16; i=i+1)
28     sb_outstate[(7+8*i):8*i]=Sbox(ctstate[(7+8*i):8*i]);
29 end
30 // ShiftRows operation
31 assign sr_outstate=ShiftR(sb_outstate);
32 // MixColumns operation
33 always @(*) begin: AESEnc_MixC
34   integer i;
35   for(i=0;i<4;i=i+1)
36     mc_outstate[(31+32*i):32*i]=
37       MixC(sr_outstate[(31+32*i):32*i]);
38 end
39 // Multiplexer
40 always @(*)
41       if(rnd_cnt==0)
42         mux_outstate=ptstate;
43   else if(rnd_cnt!=FINAL_CNT)
44         mux_outstate=mc_outstate;
45   else    mux_outstate=sr_outstate;
46 // AddRoundKey operation
47 assign ak_outstate=AddK(mux_outstate, keystate);
48 // Pipeline register
49 always @(posedge clk)
50   ctstate<=ak_outstate;
51 // Generate output control signals
52 always @(posedge clk or negedge rst_n)
53       if(!rst_n)
54         out_valid<=0;
55   else if(rnd_cnt==FINAL_CNT)
56         out_valid<=1;
57   else    out_valid<=0;
58 endmodule
```

Additionally, the original pipeline register continuously latches its D-input. By implementing the clock gating technique, the pipeline register can conditionally qualify control signals, ensuring it only latches its D-input when necessary. This helps eliminate unnecessary switching activity for both combinational and sequential circuits, and reduces power consumption.

```
1 // Pipeline register defined by clock gating
2 always @(posedge clk)
3    if(in_valid||rnd_cnt!=0)
4       ctstate<=ak_outstate;
```

Finally, the planned timing diagram is illustrated below. Once activated by the in_valid signal, the AES encryption process requires a total of 11 clock cycles. To avoid idle periods in the circuit, the control interface does not require a handshake mechanism, allowing the next input valid signal to coincide with the output valid signal. As the major processing steps of AES encryption are executed through pure combinational circuits, internal signals like sb_outstate, sr_outstate, mc_outstate, mux_outstate, and ak_outstate are omitted. To save the space, the folded AES decryption can be similarly designed and omitted as well.

In conclusion, the proposed design can be adapted in various ways depending on the desired clock frequency. For instance, a multiple-round one-cycle circuit can be designed, enabling multiple rounds to be executed within a single clock cycle to reduce the overall number of required clock cycles.

2.5 UNFOLDED DESIGN

The folded design necessitates multiple clock cycles, resulting in reduced throughput. In contrast, unfolding all rounds of AES allows for a trade-off, optimizing throughput at the expense of increased area, as presented in Figure 2.12. However, unfolding all rounds without integrating pipeline registers allows for the generation of one ciphertext per clock cycle. Nevertheless, this approach results in an excessively long critical path, significantly reducing the clock frequency. Furthermore, all round keys must also be generated within a single clock cycle.

Consequently, to improve clock frequency and thereby increase throughput, it is common to incorporate pipeline registers when unfolding all rounds of AES, as illustrated by the dashed lines in Figure 2.12.

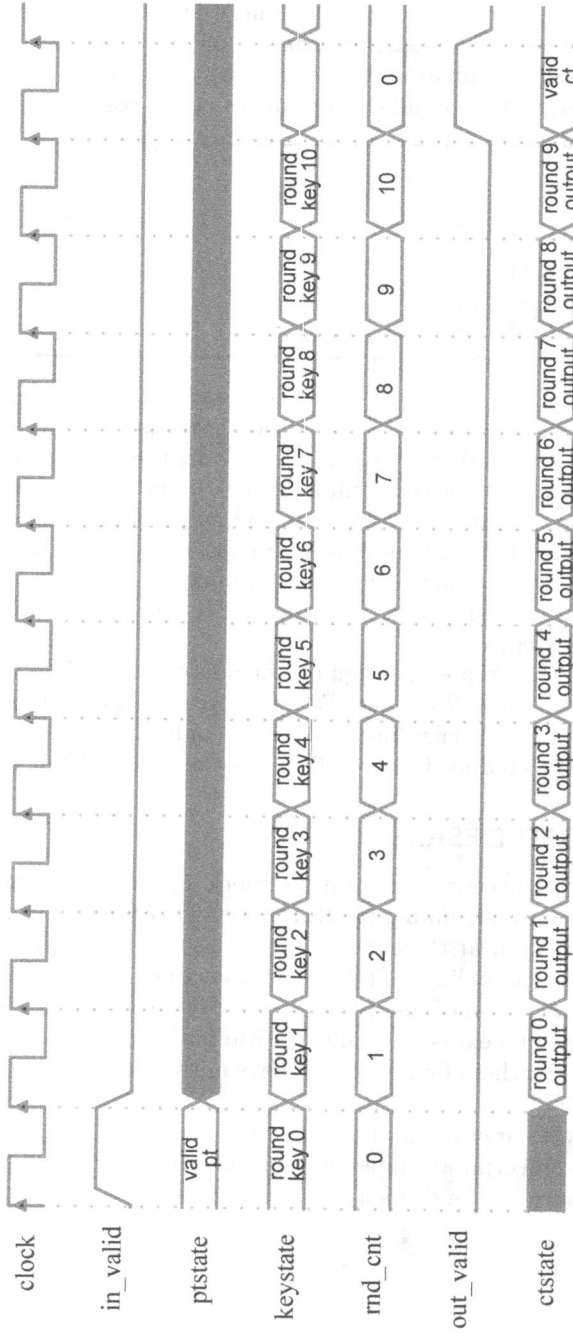

Figure 2.11: Timing diagram of folded AES single-round one-cycle design.

(a)

(b)

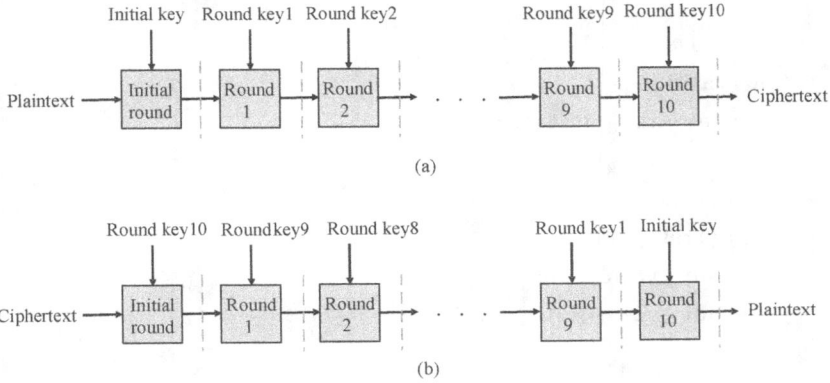

Figure 2.12: (a) Overall AES-128 encryption circuit. (b) Overall AES-128 decryption circuit.

The RTL codes for the unfolded AES encryption design, as illustrated in Figure 2.12, are detailed below. The control unit operates primarily based on the input valid (in_valid) and the output valid (out_valid) signals, and the input valid (in_valid) should be pipelined. Round keys (not shown here) need to be pipelined as well. Since all rounds are unfolded, the round counter (rnd_cnt) and multiplexers of the folded design are no longer needed. Three distinct modules for the initial (UnfoldIniRnd module), remaining (UnfoldRemRnd module), and final (UnfoldFinRnd module) rounds are designed.

```
1 // Initial round
2 module UnfoldIniRnd(out_valid, ctstate, in_valid, ptstate,
3                     keystate, clk, rst_n);
4 output out_valid;
5 output [127:0] ctstate;
6 input in_valid;
7 input [127:0] ptstate, keystate;
8 input clk, rst_n;
9 reg out_valid;
10 reg [127:0] ctstate;
11 reg [127:0] ak_outstate;
12 // AddRoundKey operation
```

```verilog
13 assign ak_outstate=AddK( ptstate , keystate );
14 // Pipeline register
15 always @( posedge clk )
16    if ( in_valid )
17      ctstate<=ak_outstate ;
18 // Generate output control signals
19 always @( posedge clk or negedge rst_n )
20         if ( ! rst_n )
21           out_valid <=0;
22    else     out_valid<=in_valid ;
23 endmodule
24 // Remaining round
25 module UnfoldRemRnd( out_valid , ctstate , in_valid , ptstate ,
26                     keystate , clk , rst_n );
27 output out_valid ;
28 output [127:0] ctstate ;
29 input in_valid ;
30 input [127:0] ptstate , keystate ;
31 input clk , rst_n ;
32 reg out_valid ;
33 reg [127:0] ctstate ;
34 reg [127:0] sb_outstate , mc_outstate ;
35 wire [127:0] sr_outstate , ak_outstate ;
36 // SubBytes operation
37 always @(*) begin : AESEnc_Sbox
38    integer i ;
39    for ( i=0; i<16; i=i+1)
40      sb_outstate [(7+8*i ) : 8* i]=Sbox( ctstate [(7+8* i ) :8* i ]);
41 end
42 // ShiftRows operation
43 assign sr_outstate=ShiftR ( sb_outstate );
44 // MixColumns operation
45 always @(*) begin : AESEnc_MixC
46    integer i ;
47    for ( i=0; i <4; i=i+1)
```

```
48      mc_outstate[(31+32*i):32*i]=
49        MixC(sr_outstate[(31+32*i):32*i]);
50 end
51 // AddRoundKey operation
52 assign ak_outstate=AddK(mc_outstate, keystate);
53 // Pipeline register
54 always @(posedge clk)
55    if(in_valid)
56      ctstate<=ak_outstate;
57 // Generate output control signals
58 always @(posedge clk or negedge rst_n)
59        if (!rst_n)
60            out_valid<=0;
61    else    out_valid<=in_valid;
62 endmodule
63 // Final round
64 module UnfoldFinRnd(out_valid, ctstate, in_valid, ptstate,
65                      keystate, clk, rst_n);
66 output out_valid;
67 output [127:0] ctstate;
68 input in_valid;
69 input [127:0] ptstate, keystate;
70 input clk, rst_n;
71 reg out_valid;
72 reg [127:0] ctstate;
73 reg [127:0] sb_outstate;
74 wire [127:0] sr_outstate, ak_outstate;
75 // SubBytes operation
76 always @(*) begin: AESEnc_Sbox
77    integer i;
78    for(i=0; i<16; i=i+1)
79      sb_outstate[(7+8*i):8*i]=Sbox(ctstate[(7+8*i):8*i]);
80 end
81 // ShiftRows operation
82 assign sr_outstate=ShiftR(sb_outstate);
```

```
83 // AddRoundKey operation
84 assign ak_outstate=AddK(sr_outstate, keystate);
85 // Pipeline register
86 always @(posedge clk)
87   if(in_valid)
88     ctstate<=ak_outstate;
89 // Generate output control signals
90 always @(posedge clk or negedge rst_n)
91       if(!rst_n)
92           out_valid<=0;
93   else      out_valid<=in_valid;
94 endmodule
```

Subsequently, they are integrated in the top module, UnfoldAESEnc, described below. We use the parameter REM_RND_NUM to define the number of remaining rounds, and it is employed by the generate statement to produce an array of instances.

```
1 // Unfolded single-round AES encryption
2 module UnfoldAESEnc #(parameter REM_RND_NUM=9)(
3         out_valid, ctstate, in_valid, ptstate,
4         keystate, clk, rst_n);
5 output out_valid;
6 output [127:0] ctstate;
7 input in_valid;
8 input [127:0] ptstate;
9 input [128*(REM_RND_NUM+2)-1:0] keystate;
10 input clk, rst_n;
11 wire out_valid;
12 wire [127:0] ctstate;
13 reg [127:0] tmp_keystate[0:(REM_RND_NUM+1)];
14 // Change linear output to byte array
15 always @(*) begin: key_linear_to_array
16   integer i;
17   for(i=0; i<(REM_RND_NUM+2); i=i+1)
```

```verilog
18        tmp_keystate[i]=keystate[(127+128*i):128*i];
19 end
20 // Instantiate initial round
21 UnfoldIniRnd UnfoldIniRnd(
22 .out_valid(ini_out_valid), .ctstate(ini_ctstate),
23 .in_valid(in_valid), .ptstate(ptstate),
24 .keystate(tmp_keystate[0]), .clk(clk), .rst_n(rst_n));
25 // Instantiate remaining rounds using generate statement
26 wire [10:0] tmp_out_valid;
27 wire [127:0] tmp_ctstate[0:10];
28 assign tmp_out_valid[0]=ini_out_valid;
29 assign tmp_ctstate[0]=ini_ctstate;
30 genvar i;
31 generate
32    for (i=0;i<REM_RND_NUM; i=i+1) begin: gen_block
33      UnfoldRemRnd u_unfoldremrnd(
34        .out_valid(tmp_out_valid[i+1]),
35        .ctstate(tmp_ctstate[i+1]),
36        .in_valid(tmp_out_valid[i]), .ptstate(tmp_ctstate[i]),
37        .keystate(tmp_keystate[i+1]), .clk(clk), .rst_n(rst_n));
38    end
39 endgenerate
40 // Instantiate final round
41 UnfoldFiniRnd UnfoldFiniRnd(
42 .out_valid(tmp_out_valid[REM_RND_NUM+1]),
43 .ctstate(tmp_ctstate[REM_RND_NUM+1]),
44 .in_valid(tmp_out_valid[REM_RND_NUM]),
45 .ptstate(tmp_ctstate[REM_RND_NUM]),
46 .keystate(tmp_keystate[REM_RND_NUM+1]),
47 .clk(clk), .rst_n(rst_n));
48 // Generate output
49 assign out_valid=tmp_out_valid[REM_RND_NUM+1];
50 assign ctstate=tmp_ctstate[REM_RND_NUM+1];
51 endmodule
```

However, while one ciphertext can be produced within a single clock cycle, this advantage comes with the drawback of increased latency. The timing diagram below demonstrates the continuous input of three plaintexts, resulting in the continuous output of three ciphertexts after 11 cycles. Disregarding the initial latency for the first ciphertext, the unfolded design produces one result per clock cycle, whereas the folded design requires 11 clock cycles to generate a single result. Notably, only the signals of I/O interface are shown to save the space.

2.6 SUB-PIPELINED DESIGN

2.6.1 AES ENCRYPTION

The maximum path delays of the initial, remaining, and final rounds of the unfolded AES design correspond to the major processing steps involved in them. However, the maximum path delays of the initial, remaining, and final rounds differ significantly. Moreover, the critical path of the unfolded AES design is located in the remaining round, determined by the path delays of SubBytes, ShiftRows, MixColumns, and AddRoundKey. As the ShiftRows operation essentially involves rewiring, it does not introduce any delay. To reduce the critical path, additional pipeline registers will be introduced, forming what is referred to as the sub-pipeline design.

To increase the clock frequency and throughput, the pipeline technique is usually adopted. In addition to shorting the critical path, making path delays balanced is the key point of pipelined circuits. In the following, we will treat the path delays of a 2-to-1 multiplexer and XOR as roughly the same. It can be observed that the S-box contains eight 256-to-1 multiplexers. Besides, a 256-to-1 multiplexer (in Figure 2.14(a)) corresponds to 8-stage 2-to-1 multiplexers (in Figure 2.14(b)), where the dashed line represents the locations registers are inserted. The stage 1 contains 128 2-to-1 multiplexers in parallel, stage 2 contains 64 2-to-1 multiplexers in parallel, and so on. Consequently, the path delays of the 8-stage pipelined S-box are balanced with only one 2-to-1 multiplexer. Extra $128 + 64 + ... + 1 = 255$ pipeline registers are needed for single-bit output of S-box.

The ShiftRows has no logic gates in it. By contrast, the 3-stage pipelined MixColumns circuit is displayed in Figure 2.15, where the dashed line represents the locations registers are inserted. Consequently, the path delays of the pipelined MixColumns are balanced with only one XOR logic gate. Extra $20 \times 8 = 160$ pipeline registers are needed for one column output the MixColumns.

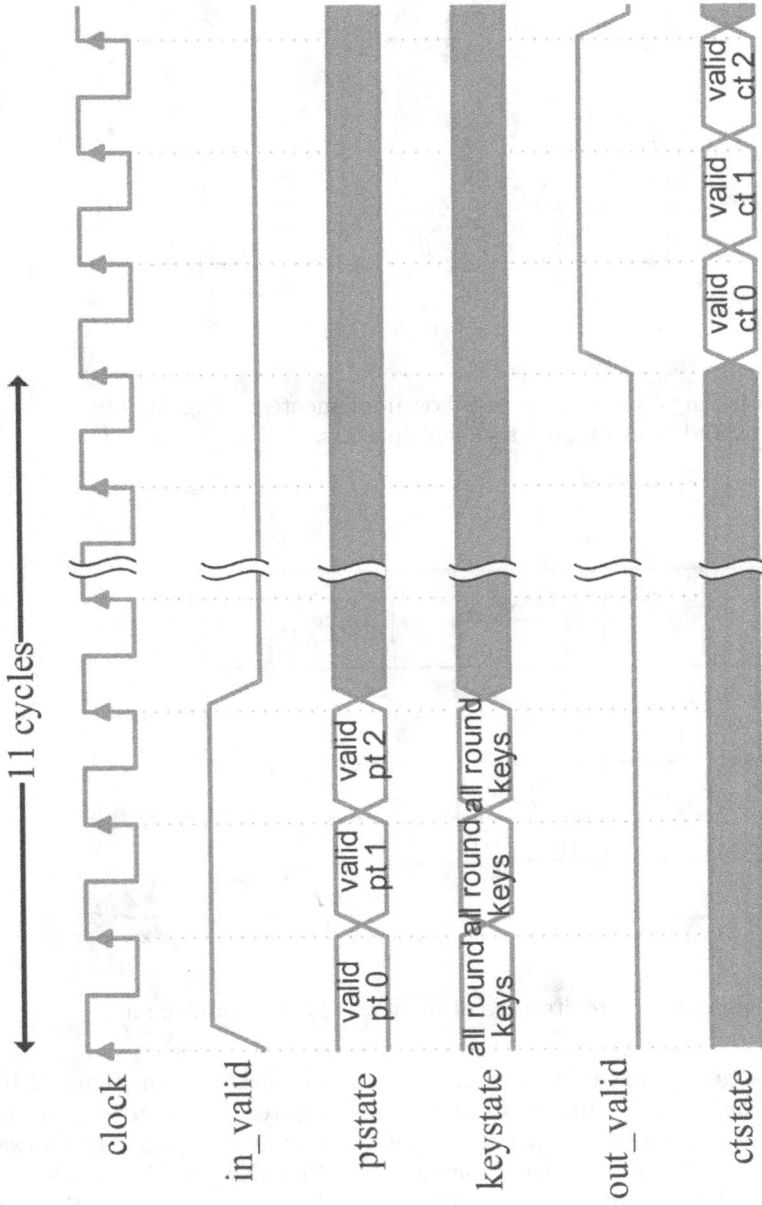

Figure 2.13: Timing diagram of unfolded AES design.

(a)

(b)

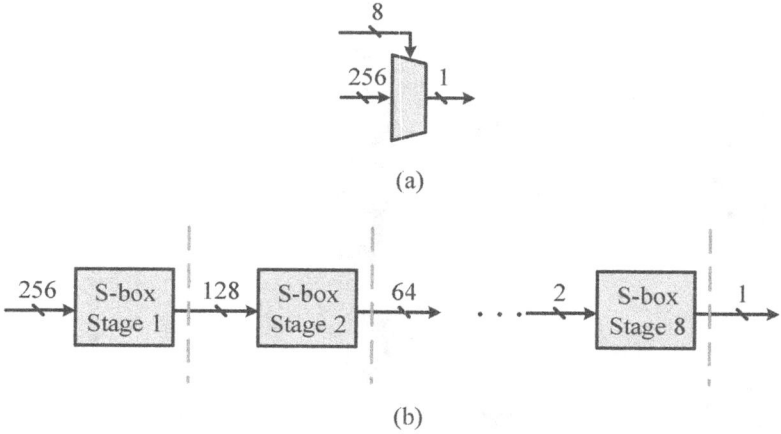

Figure 2.14: Single-bit output of S-box implemented using (a) one 256-to-1 multiplexer, and (b) 8-stage 2-to-1 multiplexers.

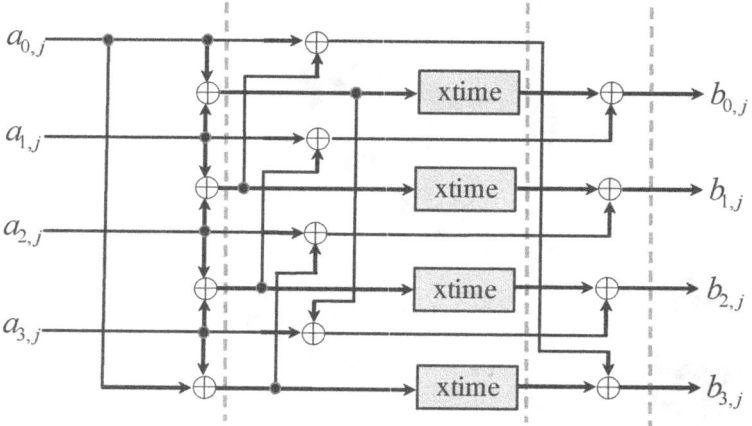

Figure 2.15: Architecture of pipelined MixColumns circuit.

The 1-stage pipelined AddRoundKey circuit is displayed in Figure 2.16, where the dashed line represents the locations registers are inserted, k is the subkey, and a and b are input and output state arrays, respectively. Consequently, the path delays of the pipelined AddRoundKey are balanced with only one XOR logic gate. Extra 128 pipeline registers are needed for the output of AddRoundKey.

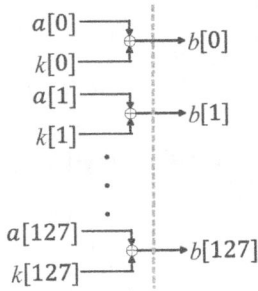

Figure 2.16: Architecture of pipelined AddRoundKey circuit.

From above, the initial round of AES encryption requires one pipeline stage for the AddRoundKey. Additionally, the remaining round circuit of AES encryption requires 14 pipeline stages, 8 for the SubBytes, 3 for the MixColumns, and 1 for the AddRoundKey. Since the final round of AES encryption does not have the MixColumns step, it requires 9 pipeline stages. In summary, the sub-pipelined AES encryption design features 136 pipeline stages, enabling the simultaneous computation of 136 ciphertexts to optimize throughput.

2.6.2 AES DECRYPTION

Similar to the S-box, it can be observed that the inverse S-box contains eight 256-to-1 multiplexers. Therefore, the architecture of S-box in Figure 2.14(b) can be applied for the inverse S-box and it is omitted here. The InvShiftRows also has no logic gates in it.

By contrast, the 6-stage pipelined InvMixColumns circuit is displayed in Figure 2.17, where the dashed line represents the locations registers are inserted. Consequently, the path delays of the pipelined InvMixColumns are balanced with only one XOR logic gate. Extra $40 \times 8 = 320$ pipeline registers are needed for one column output the InvMixColumns.

From above, the initial round of AES decryption requires one pipeline stage for the AddRoundKey. The remaining round circuit of AES decryption requires 15 pipeline stages, 8 for the InvSubBytes, 6 for the InvMixColumns, and 1 for the AddRoundKey. Additionally, since the final round of AES decryption does not have the InvMixColumns step, it requires 9 pipeline stages. In summary, the sub-pipelined AES decryption design features 145 pipeline stages, enabling the simultaneous computation of 145 plaintexts to optimize throughput.

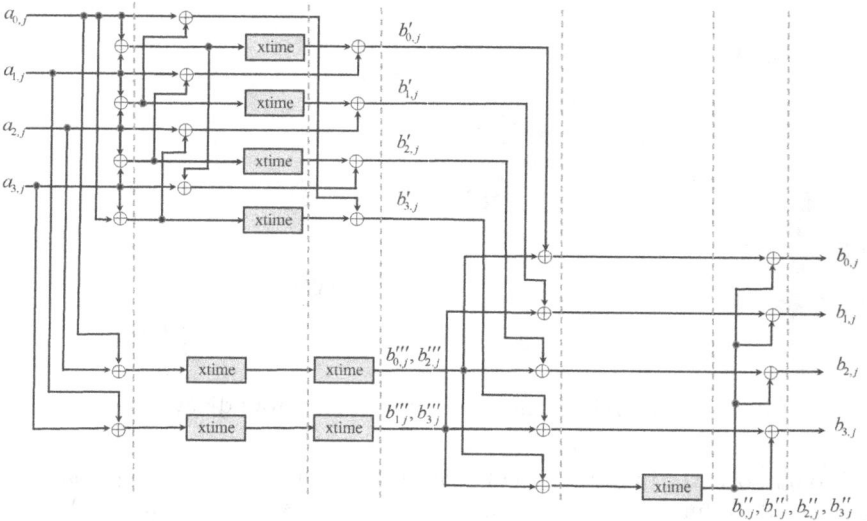

Figure 2.17: Architecture of pipelined InvMixColumns circuit.

2.7 CONSTRUCTING S-BOX USING COMPOSITE FIELD ARITHMETIC

The SubBytes and InvSubBytes operations usually occupy the largest area and exhibit the longest path delay in AES. Therefore, this section introduces an approach to reduce the required circuit area of SubBytes operation.

Using the lookup table to implement the S-box is an intuitive method, and typically, a circuit with a short critical path can be obtained. However, its circuit area will be large accordingly. By contrast, if the output of S-box is online calculated, such as using the composite field arithmetic, its circuit area will be smaller, and surely, its clock frequency will be lower as well. This situation is often encountered for most designs. That is, chip area must be traded-off for speed.

SubBytes is designed using the multiplicative inverse of input element over $GF(2^8)$ and then applying an affine transformation on the multiplicative inverse. To operate over the composite field of $GF(((2^2)^2)^2)$ for the multiplicative inverse, the element over $GF(2^8)$ must be transformed into that over $GF(((2^2)^2)^2)$ using the isomorphic mapping, δ. After the multiplicative inverse over $GF(((2^2)^2)^2)$, the element over $GF(((2^2)^2)^2)$ is converted back over $GF(2^8)$ using the inverse isomorphic mapping, δ^{-1}, as shown in Figure 2.18, where $(\cdot)^{-1}$ and AT denote the inversion and affine transformation, respectively.

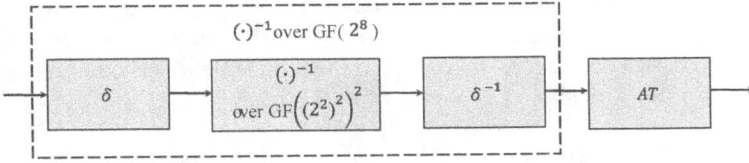

Figure 2.18: S-box implemented using composite field arithmetic.

2.7.1 ISOMORPHIC MAPPING

The isomorphic mapping is a matrix multiplication and can be written as

$$
\begin{bmatrix} p_7 \\ p_6 \\ p_5 \\ p_4 \\ p_3 \\ p_2 \\ p_1 \\ p_0 \end{bmatrix} = \begin{bmatrix} 1 & 0 & 1 & 0 & 0 & 0 & 0 & 0 \\ 1 & 1 & 0 & 1 & 1 & 1 & 1 & 0 \\ 1 & 0 & 1 & 0 & 1 & 1 & 0 & 0 \\ 1 & 0 & 1 & 0 & 1 & 1 & 1 & 0 \\ 1 & 1 & 0 & 0 & 0 & 1 & 1 & 0 \\ 1 & 0 & 0 & 1 & 1 & 1 & 1 & 0 \\ 0 & 1 & 0 & 1 & 0 & 0 & 1 & 0 \\ 0 & 1 & 0 & 0 & 0 & 1 & 1 & 1 \end{bmatrix} \begin{bmatrix} q_7 \\ q_6 \\ q_5 \\ q_4 \\ q_3 \\ q_2 \\ q_1 \\ q_0 \end{bmatrix}, \qquad (2.19)
$$

where $p = \{p_7 p_6 p_5 p_4 p_3 p_2 p_1 p_0\}_2$ and $q = \{q_7 q_6 q_5 q_4 q_3 q_2 q_1 q_0\}_2$ are respectively output and input of the isomorphic mapping, and they are elements over $GF(((2^2)^2)^2)$ and $GF(2^8)$, respectively. The isomorphic mapping can be rewritten as

$$
\begin{cases}
p_7 = q_7 + q_5 \\
p_6 = q_7 + q_6 + q_4 + q_3 + q_2 + q_1 \\
p_5 = q_7 + q_5 + q_3 + q_2 \\
p_4 = q_7 + q_5 + q_3 + q_2 + q_1 \\
p_3 = q_7 + q_6 + q_2 + q_1 \\
p_2 = q_7 + q_4 + q_3 + q_2 + q_1 \\
p_1 = q_6 + q_4 + q_1 \\
p_0 = q_6 + q_2 + q_1 + q_0
\end{cases}, \qquad (2.20)
$$

where $+$ in Galois field corresponds to the bitwise XOR operation. The isomorphic mapping requires 25 XOR gates and its critical path is three XOR gates.

2.7.2 MULTIPLICATIVE INVERSE OVER $GF(((2^2)^2)^2)$

We introduce the multiplicative inverse next. Given the irreducible polynomial, $P(x) = x^2 + Ax + B$, any polynomial can be expressed by $bx + c$ in Galois field. Besides, the multiplicative inverse of $bx + c$ can be generally written as

$$
(bx + c)^{-1} = b(b^2 B + bcA + c^2)^{-1} x + (c + bA)(b^2 B + bcA + c^2)^{-1}. \qquad (2.21)
$$

In $\mathrm{GF}(((2^2)^2)^2)$, the irreducible polynomial is $P(x) = x^2 + x + \lambda$, where $\lambda = \{1100\}_2$. Therefore, an element over $\mathrm{GF}(((2^2)^2)^2)$ can be represented using a polynomial $bx + c$, where b and c are coefficients over composite field, $\mathrm{GF}(((2^2)^2)^2)$. Specifically, the inverse of $bx + c$ over $\mathrm{GF}(((2^2)^2)^2)$ is

$$(bx+c)^{-1} = b(b^2\lambda + bc + c^2)^{-1}x + (c+b)(b^2\lambda + bc + c^2)^{-1}. \tag{2.22}$$

Table 2.4 lists irreducible polynomials over different composite fields, where $\varphi = \{10\}_2$.

Table 2.4: Irreducible polynomials.

Field	Irreducible Polynomial $P(x)$
$\mathrm{GF}(((2^2)^2)^2)$	$x^2 + x + \lambda$
$\mathrm{GF}((2^2)^2)$	$x^2 + x + \varphi$
$\mathrm{GF}(2^2)$	$x^2 + x + 1$
$\mathrm{GF}(2)$	N/A

Figure 2.19 presents the circuit architecture of the multiplicative inverse in Equation (2.22), where the 8-bit input element over $\mathrm{GF}(((2^2)^2)^2)$ is divided into two halves, the most significant high nibble (4 bits), b, and the least significant low nibble (4 bits), c, $(\cdot)^2$ denotes the squaring over $\mathrm{GF}((2^2)^2)$, $\times\lambda$ denotes multiplication with constant λ over $\mathrm{GF}((2^2)^2)$, $\times$ denotes the multiplication over $\mathrm{GF}((2^2)^2)$, and $(\cdot)^{-1}$ denotes the inversion over $\mathrm{GF}((2^2)^2)$.

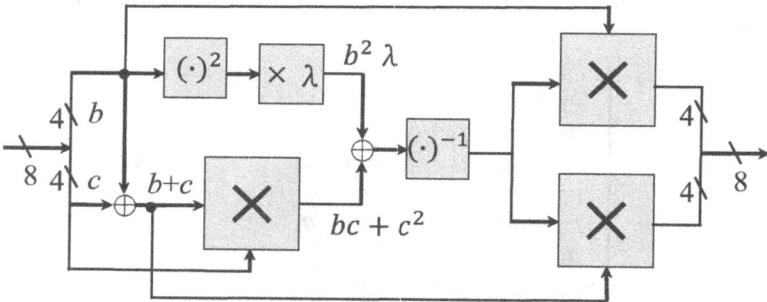

Figure 2.19: Circuit architecture of the multiplicative inverse over $\mathrm{GF}(((2^2)^2)^2)$.

2.7.3 MULTIPLICATION OVER GF$((2^2)^2)$

An element over $\mathrm{GF}((2^2)^2)$ is denoted by $k = \{k_3k_2k_1k_0\}_2$, where $k_i \in \{0,1\}$, $i = 0,1,2,3$. Let $k_H = \{k_3k_2\}_2$ and $k_L = \{k_1k_0\}_2$, then k can be written as

$$k = k_Hx + k_L. \tag{2.23}$$

Let the product $k = qw$, where q and w are also elements over $GF((2^2)^2)$. According to the irreducible polynomial, $x^2 + x + \varphi$, where $\varphi = \{10\}_2$, one has

$$
\begin{aligned}
k &= qw \\
&= (q_H x + q_L)(w_H x + w_L) \\
&= q_H w_H x^2 + (q_H w_L + q_L w_H)x + q_L w_L \\
&= (q_H w_H + q_H w_L + q_L w_H)x + q_H w_H \varphi + \\
&\quad q_L w_L.
\end{aligned}
\tag{2.24}
$$

Comparing Equations (2.23) and (2.24), one has

$$
\begin{cases}
k_H = q_H w_H + q_H w_L + q_L w_H \\
k_L = q_H w_H \varphi + q_L w_L
\end{cases}.
\tag{2.25}
$$

According to the irreducible polynomial, $x^2 + x + 1$, over $GF(2^2)$, one can further reduce Equation (2.25) by

$$
\begin{aligned}
q_H w_H &= (q_3 x + q_2)(w_3 x + w_2) \\
&= (q_3 w_3 + q_3 w_2 + q_2 w_3)x + q_3 w_3 + q_2 w_2.
\end{aligned}
\tag{2.26}
$$

Similarly, it can be shown that

$$
q_H w_L = (q_3 w_1 + q_2 w_1 + q_3 w_0)x + q_3 w_1 + q_2 w_0,
\tag{2.27}
$$

$$
q_L w_H = (q_1 w_3 + q_1 w_2 + q_0 w_3)x + q_1 w_3 + q_0 w_2,
\tag{2.28}
$$

$$
q_H w_H \varphi = (q_2 w_2 + q_2 w_3 + q_3 w_2)x + q_3 w_3 + q_2 w_3 + q_3 w_2,
\tag{2.29}
$$

$$
q_L w_L = (q_1 w_1 + q_0 w_1 + q_1 w_0)x + q_1 w_1 + q_0 w_0.
\tag{2.30}
$$

Since $k_H = k_3 x + k_2$ and $k_L = k_1 x + k_0$, substituting Equations (2.26), (2.27), (2.28), (2.29), and (2.30) into Equation (2.25) and extracting common factors in k_3, k_2, k_1, k_0, one finally has

$$
\begin{cases}
k_3 = (q_3 + q_2)(w_3 + w_2) + (q_3 + q_2)(w_1 + w_0) + \\
\quad (q_1 + q_0)(w_3 + w_2) + q_2 w_0 + q_0 w_2 + q_2 w_2 \\
k_2 = q_3 w_3 + q_3 w_1 + q_1 w_3 + q_2 w_2 + q_2 w_0 + q_0 w_2 \\
k_1 = (q_3 + q_2)(w_3 + w_2) + q_3 w_3 + \\
\quad (q_1 + q_0)(w_1 + w_0) + q_0 w_0 \\
k_0 = (q_3 + q_2)(w_3 + w_2) + q_2 w_2 + q_1 w_1 + q_0 w_0
\end{cases}.
\tag{2.31}
$$

It must be emphasized here that $+$ in Galois field corresponds to the bitwise XOR operation. As presented in Equation (2.31), only $(q_3 + q_2)$, $(q_1 + q_0)$, $(w_3 + w_2)$, $(w_1 + w_0)$, $q_3 w_3$, $q_2 w_2$, $q_1 w_1$, $q_0 w_0$, and $(q_2 w_0 + q_0 w_2)$ are needed to implement the multiplication over $GF((2^2)^2)$. As displayed in Figure 2.20, the multiplication requires 18 XOR and 12 AND gates. Its critical path has four XOR and one AND gates.

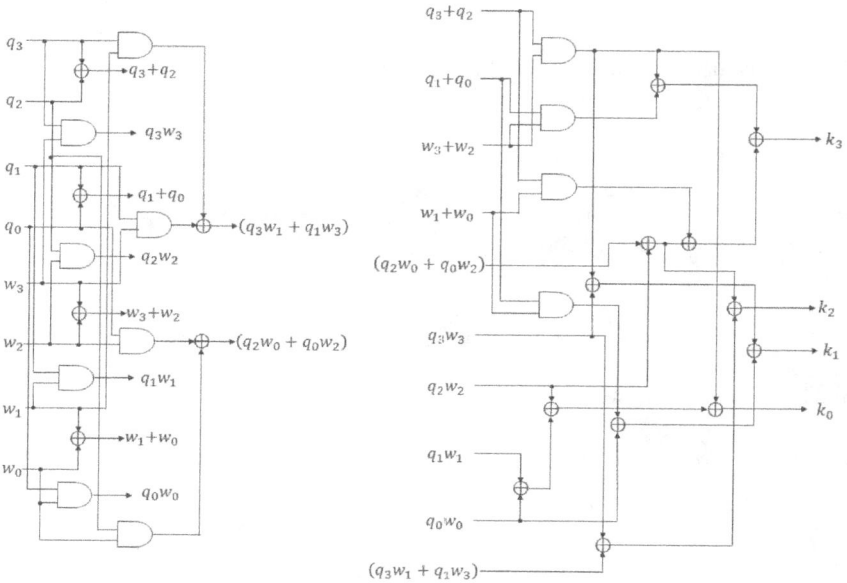

Figure 2.20: The schematic of multiplication over $GF((2^2)^2)$.

2.7.4 SQUARING AND MULTIPLICATION WITH CONSTANT λ OVER $GF((2^2)^2)$

In this section, two submodules, i.e., squaring and multiplication with constant $\lambda = \{1100\}_2$ over $GF((2^2)^2)$, are combined and optimized to improve the area efficiency. Let h be an element over $GF((2^2)^2)$, its squaring and multiplication with constant λ can be written as

$$l = \lambda h^2. \tag{2.32}$$

By the multiplication Equation (2.24) over $GF((2^2)^2)$, and knowing that $h = h_H x + h_L$ and $\lambda = \lambda_H x + \lambda_L$, Equation (2.32) can be written as

$$
\begin{aligned}
l &= (\lambda_H x + \lambda_L)(h_H x + h_L)(h_H x + h_L) \\
&= (\lambda_H x + \lambda_L)(h_H^2 x + h_H^2 \varphi + h_L^2) \\
&= (\lambda_H h_H^2 + \lambda_H h_H^2 \varphi + \lambda_H h_L^2 + \lambda_L h_H^2)x + \\
&\quad (\lambda_H h_H^2 \varphi + \lambda_L h_H^2 \varphi + \lambda_L h_L^2).
\end{aligned}
\tag{2.33}
$$

Therefore,

$$
\begin{cases}
l_H = \lambda_H h_H^2 + \lambda_H h_H^2 \varphi + \lambda_H h_L^2 + \lambda_L h_H^2 \\
l_L = \lambda_H h_H^2 \varphi + \lambda_L h_H^2 \varphi + \lambda_L h_L^2
\end{cases}.
\tag{2.34}
$$

According to the irreducible polynomial, $x^2 + x + 1$, over $GF(2^2)$ and $\lambda = \{1100\}_2$, one can further reduce Equation (2.35) and derive

$$
\begin{cases}
l_3 = h_2 + h_1 + h_0 \\
l_2 = h_3 + h_0 \\
l_1 = h_3 \\
l_0 = h_2 + h_3
\end{cases}
\tag{2.35}
$$

where l_i and h_i, $i = 0, 1, 2, 3$, are bits of elements, l and h, over $GF((2^2)^2)$, respectively. As displayed in Figure 2.21, the joint squaring and multiplication with constant λ requires four XOR gates, and its critical path has two XOR gates.

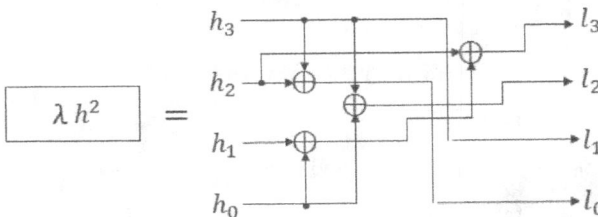

Figure 2.21: The schematic of joint squaring and multiplication with constant λ over $GF((2^2)^2)$.

2.7.5 MULTIPLICATIVE INVERSION OVER $GF((2^2)^2)$

The multiplicative inversion of y over $GF((2^2)^2)$, denoted by $y^{-1} = \{y_3^{-1} y_2^{-1} y_1^{-1} y_0^{-1}\}$, is listed in Table 2.5.

Table 2.5: The multiplicative inversion over $GF((2^2)^2)$.

Input $\{y_3y_2y_1y_0\}$	Output $\{y_3^{-1}y_2^{-1}y_1^{-1}y_0^{-1}\}$
0000	0000
0001	0001
0010	0011
0011	0010
0100	1111
0101	1100
0110	1001
0111	1011
1000	1010
1001	0110
1010	1000
1011	0111
1100	0101
1101	1110
1110	1101
1111	0100

The Boolean equations can be manually derived using the Karnaugh map (omitted here), and they are

$$
\begin{cases}
y_3^{-1} = \overline{y_3}y_2 + y_2\overline{y_1}y_0 + y_2y_1\overline{y_0} + y_3\overline{y_2}\ \overline{y_0} \\
y_2^{-1} = \overline{y_3}y_2\overline{y_1} + y_3y_2 + y_3\overline{y_2}y_0 \\
y_1^{-1} = \overline{y_1}\ \overline{y_3}y_2\overline{y_0} + \overline{y_1}y_3\overline{y_2} + y_3y_0\overline{y_1} + y_3y_0\overline{y_2} + \\
\qquad \overline{y_3}y_1\overline{y_2} + \overline{y_3}y_1y_0 \\
y_0^{-1} = \overline{y_3}y_1\overline{y_0} + \overline{y_3}y_1y_2 + \overline{y_2}y_0y_3y_1 + \overline{y_2}y_0\overline{y_3}\ \overline{y_1} + \\
\qquad y_2\overline{y_0}
\end{cases}
\tag{2.36}
$$

where the $\overline{(\cdot)}$ and $+$ respectively denote the bitwise NOT and OR. The multiplicative inversion can be shown to have logic gates including 5 INV+7 OR+2 AND+9 NAND+1 NOR+1 XOR+1 XNOR, and its critical path has logic gates including 1 XNOR+1 OR+2 INV+1 NAND+1 NOR+1 AND.

2.7.6 JOINT INVERSE ISOMORPHIC MAPPING AND AFFINE TRANSFORMATION

The inverse isomorphic mapping is a matrix multiplication and can be written as

$$
\begin{bmatrix} p_7 \\ p_6 \\ p_5 \\ p_4 \\ p_3 \\ p_2 \\ p_1 \\ p_0 \end{bmatrix} =
\begin{bmatrix}
1 & 1 & 1 & 0 & 0 & 0 & 1 & 0 \\
0 & 1 & 0 & 0 & 0 & 1 & 0 & 0 \\
0 & 1 & 1 & 0 & 0 & 0 & 1 & 0 \\
0 & 1 & 1 & 1 & 0 & 1 & 1 & 0 \\
0 & 0 & 1 & 1 & 1 & 1 & 1 & 0 \\
1 & 0 & 0 & 1 & 1 & 1 & 1 & 0 \\
0 & 0 & 1 & 1 & 0 & 0 & 0 & 0 \\
0 & 1 & 1 & 1 & 0 & 1 & 0 & 1
\end{bmatrix}
\begin{bmatrix} k_7 \\ k_6 \\ k_5 \\ k_4 \\ k_3 \\ k_2 \\ k_1 \\ k_0 \end{bmatrix},
\tag{2.37}
$$

where $p = \{p_7 p_6 p_5 p_4 p_3 p_2 p_1 p_0\}_2$ and $k = \{k_7 k_6 k_5 k_4 k_3 k_2 k_1 k_0\}_2$ are respectively output and input of the inverse isomorphic mapping, and they are elements over $GF(2^8)$ and $GF(((2^2)^2)^2)$, respectively.

The affine transformation is a linear transformation of input element over $GF(2^8)$ and can be written as

$$
\begin{bmatrix} r_7 \\ r_6 \\ r_5 \\ r_4 \\ r_3 \\ r_2 \\ r_1 \\ r_0 \end{bmatrix} =
\begin{bmatrix}
1 & 1 & 1 & 1 & 1 & 0 & 0 & 0 \\
0 & 1 & 1 & 1 & 1 & 1 & 0 & 0 \\
0 & 0 & 1 & 1 & 1 & 1 & 1 & 0 \\
0 & 0 & 0 & 1 & 1 & 1 & 1 & 1 \\
1 & 0 & 0 & 0 & 1 & 1 & 1 & 1 \\
1 & 1 & 0 & 0 & 0 & 1 & 1 & 1 \\
1 & 1 & 1 & 0 & 0 & 0 & 1 & 1 \\
1 & 1 & 1 & 1 & 0 & 0 & 0 & 1
\end{bmatrix}
\begin{bmatrix} p_7 \\ p_6 \\ p_5 \\ p_4 \\ p_3 \\ p_2 \\ p_1 \\ p_0 \end{bmatrix} +
\begin{bmatrix} 0 \\ 1 \\ 1 \\ 0 \\ 0 \\ 0 \\ 1 \\ 1 \end{bmatrix},
\tag{2.38}
$$

where $r = \{r_7 r_6 r_5 r_4 r_3 r_2 r_1 r_0\}_2$ and $p = \{p_7 p_6 p_5 p_4 p_3 p_2 p_1 p_0\}_2$ are respectively output and input of the affine transformation.

Putting Equation (2.37) into Equation (2.38) and expanding the equation, one can finally obtain

$$
\begin{cases}
r_7 = t_6 + k_3 \\
r_6 = t_5 + t_3 + 1 \\
r_5 = t_6 + 1 \\
r_4 = t_7 + k_4 + k_1 \\
r_3 = t_1 + k_0 \\
r_2 = t_8 + t_2 \\
r_1 = t_7 + 1 \\
r_0 = t_5 + t_1 + k_0 + 1
\end{cases}
\tag{2.39}
$$

where "+" is the addition in $GF((2^2)^2)$, $t_8 = t_4 + t_0$, $t_7 = k_7 + k_0$, $t_6 = k_7 + k_2$, $t_5 = k_7 + k_6$, $t_4 = k_6 + k_5$, $t_3 = k_5 + k_4$, $t_2 = k_4 + k_3$, $t_1 = k_2 + k_1$, and $t_0 = k_2 + k_0$. The joint design of inverse isomorphic mapping and affine transformation requires 25 XOR gates, and its critical path has three XOR gates.

2.8   CIPHER BLOCK CHAINING MODE OF OPERATION

In cryptography, a block cipher mode of operation is an algorithm that uses a block cipher to provide enhanced information security such as confidentiality or authenticity. A block cipher is able to encrypt one fixed-length group of bits called a block. However, a mode of operation enables us to repeatedly apply a cipher's single-block operation to securely encrypt amounts of data larger than a block. The block cipher modes operate on whole blocks and require that the last part of the data be padded to a full block if it is smaller than the block size.

With the development of communication technology, not only the high data throughput rate is an important issue, but data security is also highly noticed. The cipher-block chaining (CBC) mode is considered to be more secure than traditional electronic codebook (ECB) mode. Therefore, how to realize the AES-CBC circuit with high throughput has become an essential issue. The CBC operation mode for encryption is presented in Figure 2.22, where N denotes the number of blocks and ENC denotes the encryption. Each block of plaintext is exclusively-ORed (XORed) with the previous ciphertext block before being encrypted. Consequently, each ciphertext block relies on all plaintext blocks processed up to that point. An initialization vector must be used in the first block to make each message unique.

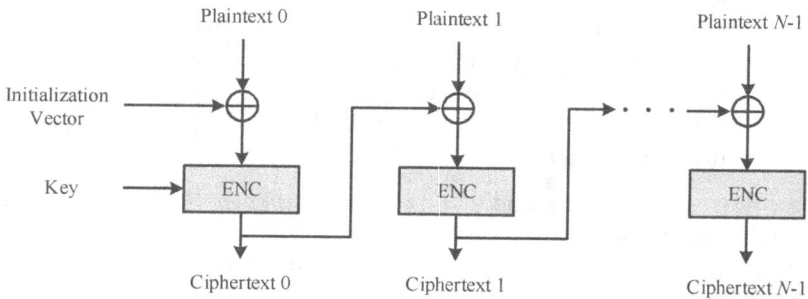

Figure 2.22: CBC operation mode of encryption.

The operation mode of CBC for decryption is presented in Figure 2.23, where N denotes the number of blocks and DEC denotes the decryption. The decryption is the reverse process of encryption. Each block of ciphertext is decrypted, and then XORed with the previous ciphertext block (the first block is XORed with the initialization vector).

Even the pipelining and unfolding techniques can increase the throughput of single AES, the performance of CBC operation mode cannot be enhanced owing to the dependency of the output of current clock on the previous block. Specifically, the encryption of current clock must be paused until the ciphertext of previous block is available, as the scheduling shown in Figure 2.24,

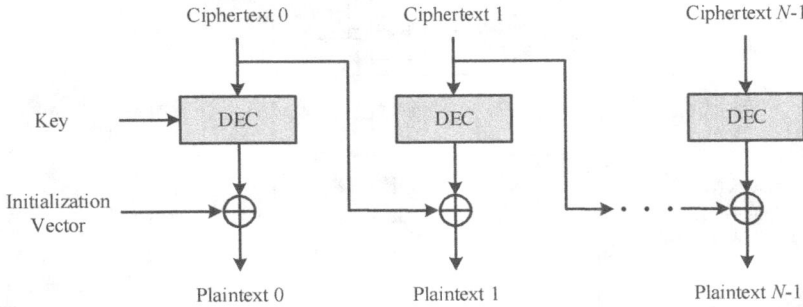

Figure 2.23: CBC operation mode of decryption.

where pt and ct denote plaintext and ciphertext, respectively, and the encryption is assumed to have three pipeline stages. As shown, despite the encryption circuit being both pipelined and unfolded, data dependency causes an output to be generated every three cycles, even though plaintexts can be supplied on every cycle.

	cycle1	cycle2	cycle3	cycle4	cycle5	cycle6	cycle7	cycle8
stage1	pt0	pt1	pt1	pt1	pt2	pt2	pt2	pt3
stage2		pt0			pt1			pt2
stage3			pt0			pt1		
output				ct0			ct1	

Figure 2.24: Scheduling of a 3-stage pipelined encryption under the CBC operation mode.

To improve the throughput of CBC operation mode, the parallel architecture is intuitively adopted in Figure 2.25(a). In order to encrypt multiple independent network channels at the same time, multiple sets of pipelined circuits are used in parallel. To maintain the same throughput as the parallel architecture while reducing the required chip area, independent network channels are multiplexed using the folded architecture in Figure 2.25(b). Only one copy of pipelined circuit is required to encrypt the data of multiple network channels at the same time. As displayed, the pipeline resources are not fully utilized by the parallel scheme. By contrast, the folded architecture fully utilizes all pipeline stages. To employ all pipeline stages, the number of multiplexed channels should equal the number of pipeline stages.

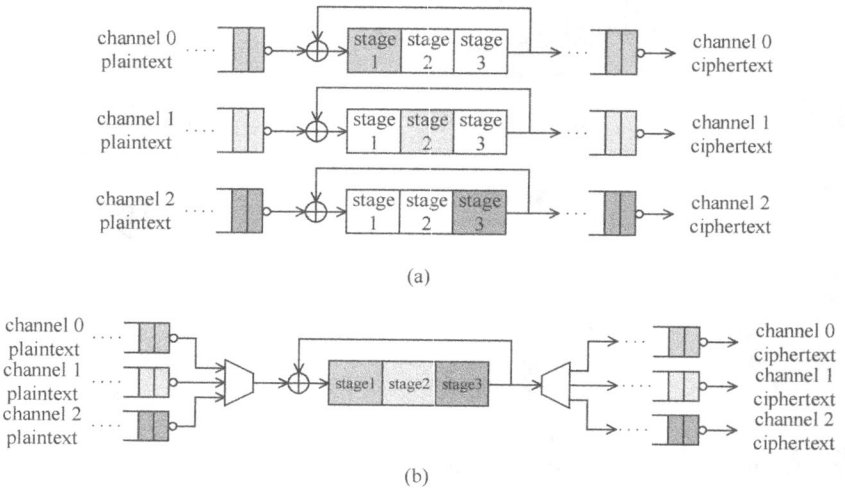

(a)

(b)

Figure 2.25: Pipelined architectures of CBC mode: (a) parallel, (b) folded.

The complete folded architecture of CBC operation mode is composed of three parts: input (demultiplexing and multiplexing), crypto engine, and output (demultiplexing and multiplexing), as shown in Figure 2.26, where C denotes the channel number, N denotes the number of pipeline stages, and N_c denotes the subchannel number of the c-th channel, $c = 0, 1, ..., C - 1$. Each subchannel will occupy a pipeline stage. Therefore, to fully utilize all pipeline stages, the total number of subchannels equal the number of pipeline stages, i.e., $N = \sum_{c=0}^{C-1} N_c$.

The input part schedules and arranges the input sequence of plaintext without needing to wait until the previous ciphertext has been completely encrypted. In addition, we can use it to flexibly allocate the hardware resources of the pipelined circuit to each network channel according to the allocated number of subchannels, N_c. As a result, the encryption speeds of all channels are proportional to $N_0:N_1:...:N_{C-1}$. Then the packet data of all subchannels will be sequentially fed into the pipelined crypto engine. Finally, the output part demultiplexes the output of crypto engine into subchannels, and then subsequently multiplexes subchannels belonging to a channel into it.

The proposed scheme can be broadly applied to other block cipher modes of operation that utilize feedback architectures. To effectively implement multiple first-in, first-out (FIFO) queues, a shared buffer design can be utilized, enabling dynamic allocation of memory space across all network channels. The shared buffer can be efficiently implemented utilizing the dynamic linked list data structure. The intricate details of this design, however, fall beyond the scope of this book.

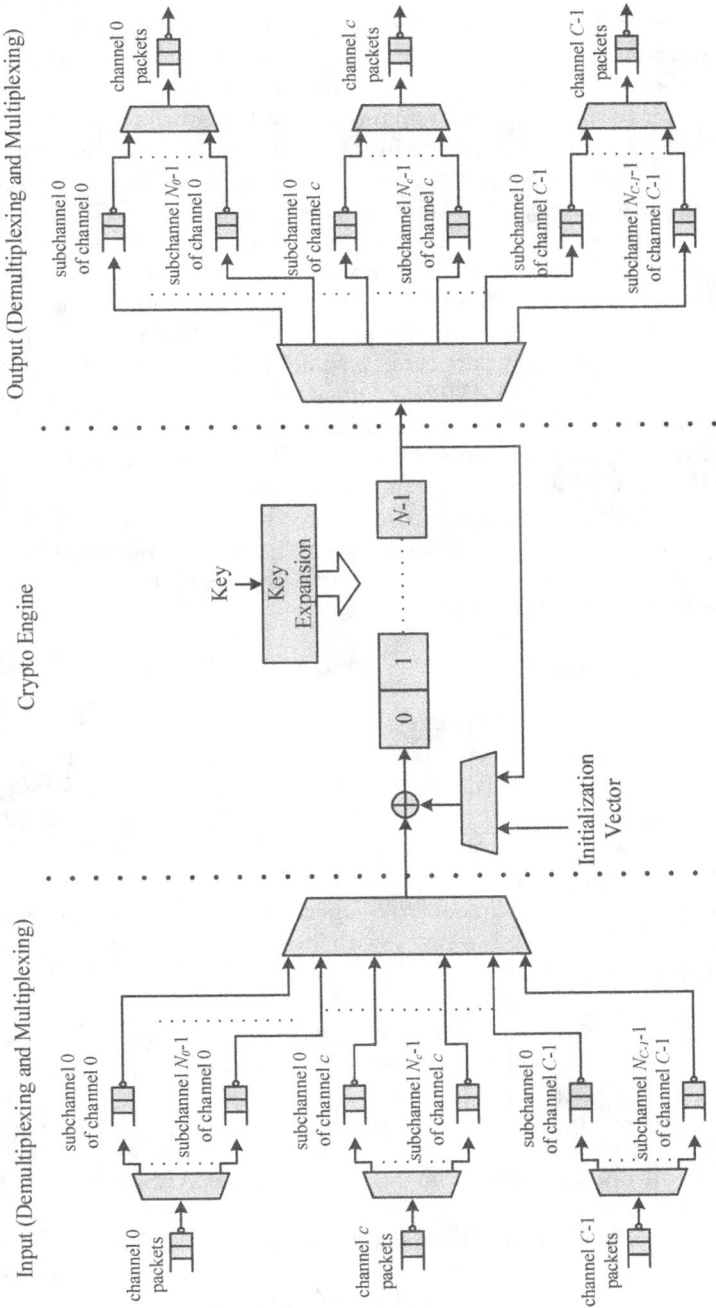

Figure 2.26: The complete folded architecture for the CBC mode of operation.

2.9 POST-QUANTUM CRYPTOGRAPHY

In the context of post-quantum cryptography (PQC), the AES continues to play a significant role, despite its primary classification as a symmetric encryption algorithm. While PQC mainly emphasizes quantum-resistant public key encryption techniques, AES remains relevant for various reasons.

Firstly, AES is considered secure in the short term, even with the potential emergence of quantum computing. Quantum attacks, such as Grover's algorithm, reduce the complexity of key searching from 2^n to $2^{n/2}$. To counter this, employing longer keys, such as 256-bit keys, ensures AES's resilience against such threats. Secondly, AES serves as a vital component in hybrid encryption systems during the transitional phase toward PQC. By integrating AES with quantum-resistant public key encryption algorithms, these systems provide an additional layer of security, particularly while quantum computers remain in developmental stages. Lastly, AES remains critical for ensuring data integrity and authentication, especially through its modes like Galois/Counter mode (GCM) of operation. These functions are indispensable in a PQC environment, where robust data validation is paramount.

In essence, AES complements quantum-resistant techniques by providing symmetric encryption security and aiding the gradual transition to a fully PQC-ready infrastructure. This dual role underscores its ongoing significance in the cryptographic landscape.

2.9.1 RIJNDAEL-256

Rijndael-256 is an advanced symmetric key encryption algorithm, developed also by Belgian cryptographers, Vincent Rijmen and Joan Daemen. It is a variant of the Rijndael family, which was selected as the basis for the AES standard by the NIST in 2001. While AES restricts the block size to 128 bits, Rijndael-256 allows for a block size of 256 bits, offering greater flexibility and security in certain applications.

Compared to AES, the Rijndael-256 algorithm operates on a state matrix organized as 8 columns and 4 rows, with each cell representing a byte, as shown in Equation (4.12),

$$\begin{bmatrix} a_{0,0} & a_{0,1} & a_{0,2} & a_{0,3} & a_{0,4} & a_{0,5} & a_{0,6} & a_{0,7} \\ a_{1,0} & a_{1,1} & a_{1,2} & a_{1,3} & a_{1,4} & a_{1,5} & a_{1,6} & a_{1,7} \\ a_{2,0} & a_{2,1} & a_{2,2} & a_{2,3} & a_{2,4} & a_{2,5} & a_{2,6} & a_{2,7} \\ a_{3,0} & a_{3,1} & a_{3,2} & a_{3,3} & a_{3,4} & a_{3,5} & a_{3,6} & a_{3,7} \end{bmatrix} \tag{2.40}$$

where $a_{i,j}$ is an 8-bit binary number, called state in AES, $i = 0, 1, 2, 3$, and $j = 0, 1, 2, 3, 4, 5, 6, 7$.

Rijndael-256 offers greater flexibility by allowing both the block size and key size to be independently chosen. Block sizes and key sizes can be 128, 192, or 256 bits, meaning Rijndael-256 supports larger block sizes, such as 256 bits, which are not part of AES's design. In contrast, AES standardizes the block size to 128 bits while allowing key sizes of 128, 192, or 256 bits. This standardization makes AES simpler and more optimized for hardware and software implementation, contributing to its widespread adoption.

Rijndael-256 employs a series of transformations similar to AES, including SubBytes, ShiftRows, MixColumns, and AddRoundKey. These transformations are repeated over 14 rounds for a 256-bit key, ensuring robust encryption. One of the unique features of Rijndael-256 is its ability to independently specify both the block size and key size, which can be 128, 192, or 256 bits. This flexibility makes it suitable for a wide range of cryptographic applications, from securing communications to protecting sensitive data in storage.

Although Rijndael-256 is not as widely adopted as AES due to its larger block size, it remains an important cryptographic tool, particularly in scenarios requiring enhanced security. Its design principles and mathematical rigor continue to influence modern encryption standards, such as PQC. In terms of security, both algorithms are robust. However, Rijndael-256's support for a 256-bit block size offers additional security against certain types of attacks, such as meet-in-the-middle attacks, where an attacker might exploit smaller block sizes. Despite this, AES is considered highly secure and practical for most real-world scenarios.

Performance is another point of distinction. The larger block size of Rijndael-256 can provide stronger security but at the cost of slower performance, especially in hardware-constrained environments. AES, with its fixed 128-bit block size, is faster and more efficient, which is one reason it became the encryption standard for many applications.

3 Data Encryption Standard

The data encryption standard (DES) algorithm is a symmetric key encryption algorithm developed by IBM, which was later adopted as a data processing standard by the National Institute of Standards and Technology (NIST) in 1977. DES played a significant role in the history of cryptography, becoming one of the most widely used encryption methods during its time.

At its inception, DES was celebrated for its innovative design and ability to provide a standardized approach to encryption. It introduced key cryptographic concepts, such as S-boxes and the Feistel structure, which continue to influence modern algorithms. DES became the foundation for secure data transmission in financial, governmental, and commercial sectors. Its hardware efficiency also made it popular for applications requiring high-speed encryption.

Despite its initial success, DES's 56-bit key length became a liability over time. Actually, the key length of DES is 64 bits. However, only 56 bits of the key are effectively used for encryption, as 8 bits are reserved for parity checks. This results in a key space of 2^{56} possible keys. Advances in computational power rendered brute-force attacks feasible, demonstrating that DES was no longer sufficient for protecting sensitive information. By the late 1990s, DES was effectively broken when researchers performed key recovery attacks within a practical timeframe.

As a response, triple data encryption algorithm (TDEA or 3DES) was introduced, extending the effective key length by encrypting data three times with DES using different keys. However, 3DES was later phased out in favor of the advanced encryption standard (AES), which offers greater security, efficiency, and scalability.

DES remains an important milestone in the evolution of cryptography. Although it is no longer recommended for secure communications, its design principles continue to inform modern encryption methods. For cryptographic researchers and enthusiasts, DES serves as a textbook example of both innovation and the need for continual adaptation in the face of evolving threats.

3.1 INTRODUCTION

DES operates by encrypting 64-bit blocks of data using a 56-bit key through a series of 16 rounds, each involving substitutions, permutations, and XOR operations within a Feistel network structure. The process begins with an initial permutation of the plaintext, followed by iterative transformations where a unique subkey is applied in each round. After the rounds, a final permutation produces the ciphertext. This structured approach, combined with efficient

DOI: 10.1201/9781003650553-3

key scheduling, allows DES to provide secure data encryption, though its key length is now considered insufficient against modern computational attacks.

The advantage of its structure is that the operations of encryption and decryption are very similar. The only difference is that the order of the subkeys used for encryption and decryption is reversed.

Specifically, DES operates on a whole block and requires that the data be padded to a full block if it is smaller than the block size. DES data are divided into fixed 64-bit data blocks. It is an iterative algorithm and uses a round function for 16 times. The DES encryption algorithm is presented in Figure 3.1 and it is also called Feistel cipher, where the IP, F_i, $i = 1, 2, ..., 16$, and FP are initial permutation, F blocks, and final permutation, respectively. The plaintext is first rearranged by the initial permutation, and then divided into two 32-bit half blocks on the left and right, and then 16 rounds of operations are performed. The round function contains F block and XOR operation.

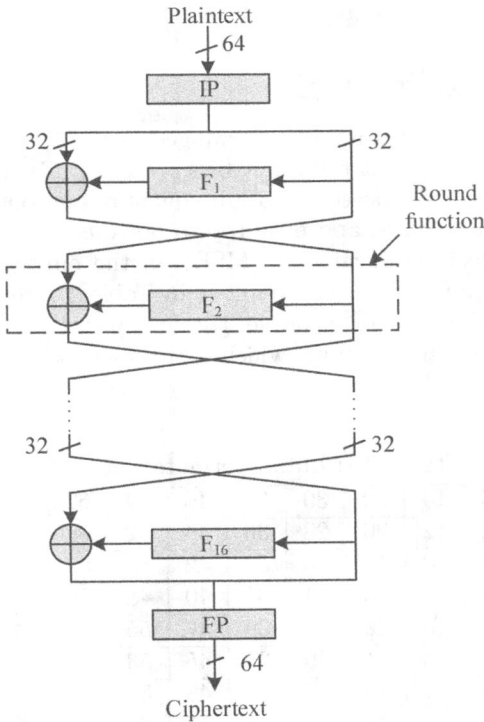

Figure 3.1: Flow chart of DES encryption algorithm.

The F block is displayed in Figure 3.2 and contains four steps: expansion (E), XOR operation for subkey mixing, substitution box (S-box), and permutation (P).

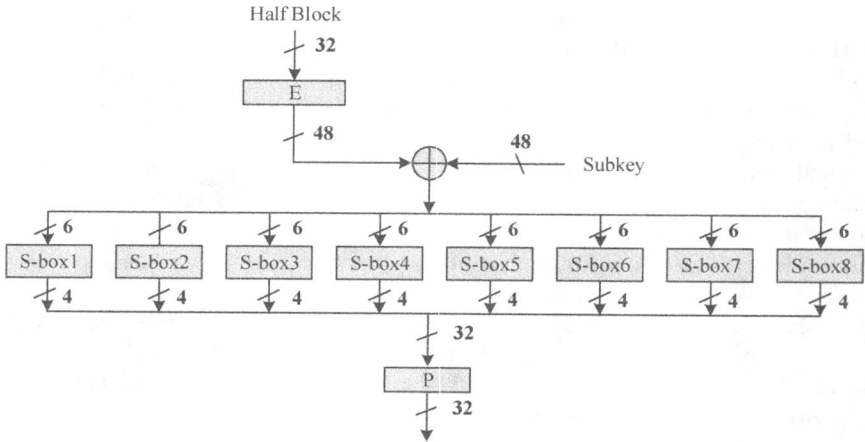

Figure 3.2: F block.

3.2 INITIAL PERMUTATION

The input plaintext is broken up and rearranged as that shown in Table 3.1. This permutation ensures that the input bits are reorganized as required by the DES algorithm before proceeding to subsequent operations. The locations in the table from left to right, and from top to bottom, represent those from the 63rd bit, i.e., most significant bit (MSB), of the output to its 0th bit, i.e., least significant bit (LSB). The number in Table 3.1 represents the bit position of input plaintext. For example, the first position in the upper left corner is the 63rd bit of the output, which corresponds to the 6th bit of the plaintext.

Table 3.1: Initial permutation.

6	14	22	30	38	46	54	62
4	12	20	28	36	44	52	60
2	10	18	26	34	42	50	58
0	8	16	24	32	40	48	56
7	15	23	31	39	47	55	63
5	13	21	29	37	45	53	61
3	11	19	27	35	43	51	59
1	9	17	25	33	41	49	57

The RTL code of initial permutation is written below, where in and out signals are 64-bit input and output of the initial permutation, respectively. The initial permutation is implemented using rewiring without any logic gates.

```
1// Initial permutation
2 wire [63 : 0] in ;
3 wire [63 : 0] out ;
4 assign out={in [6] , in [14] , in [22] , in [30] , in [38] , in [46] ,
5           in [54] , in [62] ,
6           in [4] , in [12] , in [20] , in [28] , in [36] , in [44] ,
7           in [52] , in [60] ,
8           in [2] , in [10] , in [18] , in [26] , in [34] , in [42] ,
9           in [50] , in [58] ,
10          in [0] , in [8] , in [16] , in [24] , in [32] , in [40] ,
11          in [48] , in [56] ,
12          in [7] , in [15] , in [23] , in [31] , in [39] , in [47] ,
13          in [55] , in [63] ,
14          in [5] , in [13] , in [21] , in [29] , in [37] , in [45] ,
15          in [53] , in [61] ,
16          in [3] , in [11] , in [19] , in [27] , in [35] , in [43] ,
17          in [51] , in [59] ,
18          in [1] , in [9] , in [17] , in [25] , in [33] , in [41] ,
19          in [49] , in [57] };
```

3.3 F BLOCK

3.3.1 EXPANSION

The 32-bit input is expanded to 48-bit output as that shown in Table 3.2. The expansion operation takes a 32-bit input and expands it to a 48-bit output by duplicating certain bits according to the standard DES Expansion table. The expansion function not only increases the input size but also introduces non-linear bit dependencies, enhancing diffusion. The locations in the table from left to right, and from top to bottom, represent those from the 47th bit, i.e., MSB, of the output to its 0th bit, i.e., LSB. The number in Table 3.2 represents the bit position of input. For example, the first position in the upper left corner is the 47th bit of the output, which corresponds to the 0th bit of the input.

Table 3.2: Expansion.

0	31	30	29	28	27
28	27	26	25	24	23
24	23	22	21	20	19
20	19	18	17	16	15
16	15	14	13	12	11
12	11	10	9	8	7
8	7	6	5	4	3
4	3	2	1	0	31

The RTL code of expansion is written below, where in and out signals are 32-bit input and 48-bit output of the expansion function, respectively. The expansion is implemented using rewiring without any logic gates.

```
1 // Expansion
2 wire [31:0] in;
3 wire [47:0] out;
4 assign out={in[0], in[31], in[30], in[29], in[28], in[27],
5             in[28], in[27], in[26], in[25], in[24], in[23],
6             in[24], in[23], in[22], in[21], in[20], in[19],
7             in[20], in[19], in[18], in[17], in[16], in[15],
8             in[16], in[15], in[14], in[13], in[12], in[11],
9             in[12], in[11], in[10], in[9], in[8], in[7],
10            in[8], in[7], in[6], in[5], in[4], in[3],
11            in[4], in[3], in[2], in[1], in[0], in[31]};
```

3.3.2 SUBKEY MIXING

The RTL code of the XOR operation for subkey mixing is written below, where key signal is 48-bit subkey, and in and out signals are 48-bit input and output, respectively.

```
1 // Subkey mixing implemented using XOR gates
2 wire [47:0] in, key, out;
3 assign out=in^key;
```

3.3.3 SUBSTITUTION BOX

After the subkey mixing operation, a 48-bit data can be obtained. Then this data will be divided into eight 6-bit groups, and each group of data has a corresponding substitution box or S-box. There are eight S-boxes in the F block, as shown in Tables 3.3–3.10, where all values are represented in hexadecimal. Every S-box properly maps each 6-bit input to its corresponding 4-bit output based on the predefined S-box substitution values. The row of S-box is determined by the MSB and LSB of input, and the column is determined by remaining middle bits. For example, if the input of S-box 1 is 101100_2, the row index of S-box is 10_2 and the column index is 0110_2. Therefore, the 4-bit output of S-box is 4'b0010. The 4-bit outputs of all eight S-boxes are finally combined into a 32-bit data.

Table 3.3: S-box 1.

	0	1	2	3	4	5	6	7	8	9	a	b	c	d	e	f
0	e	4	d	1	2	f	b	8	3	a	6	c	5	9	0	7
1	0	f	7	4	e	2	d	1	a	6	c	b	9	5	3	8
2	4	1	e	8	d	6	2	b	f	c	9	7	3	a	5	0
3	f	c	8	2	4	9	1	7	5	b	3	e	a	0	6	d

Table 3.4: S-box 2.

	0	1	2	3	4	5	6	7	8	9	a	b	c	d	e	f
0	f	1	8	e	6	b	3	4	9	7	2	d	c	0	5	a
1	3	d	4	7	f	2	8	1	a	6	c	b	9	5	3	8
2	0	e	7	b	a	4	d	1	5	8	c	6	9	3	2	f
3	d	8	a	1	3	f	4	2	b	6	7	c	0	5	e	9

Table 3.5: S-box 3.

	0	1	2	3	4	5	6	7	8	9	a	b	c	d	e	f
0	a	0	9	e	6	3	f	5	1	d	c	7	b	4	2	8
1	d	7	0	9	3	4	6	a	2	8	5	e	c	b	f	1
2	d	6	4	9	8	f	3	0	b	1	2	c	5	a	e	7
3	1	a	d	0	6	9	8	7	4	f	e	3	b	5	2	c

Table 3.6: S-box 4.

	0	1	2	3	4	5	6	7	8	9	a	b	c	d	e	f
0	7	d	e	3	0	6	9	a	1	2	8	5	b	c	4	f
1	d	8	b	5	6	f	0	3	4	7	2	c	1	a	e	9
2	a	6	9	0	c	b	7	d	f	1	3	e	5	2	8	4
3	3	f	0	6	a	1	d	8	9	4	5	b	c	7	2	e

Table 3.7: S-box 5.

	0	1	2	3	4	5	6	7	8	9	a	b	c	d	e	f
0	2	c	4	1	7	a	b	6	8	5	3	f	d	0	e	9
1	e	b	2	c	4	7	d	1	5	0	f	a	3	9	8	6
2	4	2	1	b	a	d	7	8	f	9	c	5	6	3	0	e
3	b	8	c	7	1	e	2	d	6	f	0	9	a	4	5	3

Table 3.8: S-box 6.

	0	1	2	3	4	5	6	7	8	9	a	b	c	d	e	f
0	c	1	a	f	9	2	6	8	0	d	3	4	e	7	5	b
1	a	f	4	2	7	c	9	5	6	1	d	e	0	b	3	8
2	9	e	f	5	2	8	c	3	7	0	4	a	1	d	b	6
3	4	3	2	c	9	5	f	a	b	e	1	7	6	0	8	d

Table 3.9: S-box 7.

	0	1	2	3	4	5	6	7	8	9	a	b	c	d	e	f
0	4	b	2	e	f	0	8	d	3	c	9	7	5	a	6	1
1	d	0	b	7	4	9	1	a	e	3	5	c	2	f	8	6
2	1	4	b	d	c	3	7	e	a	f	6	8	0	5	9	2
3	6	b	d	8	1	4	a	7	9	5	0	f	e	2	3	c

Table 3.10: S-box 8.

	0	1	2	3	4	5	6	7	8	9	a	b	c	d	e	f
0	d	2	8	4	6	f	b	1	a	9	3	e	5	0	c	7
1	1	f	d	8	a	3	7	4	c	5	6	b	0	e	9	2
2	7	b	4	1	9	c	e	2	0	6	a	d	f	3	5	8
3	2	1	e	7	4	a	8	d	f	c	9	0	3	5	6	b

Intuitively, the S-box 1 (and other S-boxes) can be implemented using a lookup table, described using a Verilog function as follows. The in signal and Sbox1 (function name) are the input and output of the function, respectively. The lookup table is essentially a 64-to-1 multiplexer.

```
1 // S-box implemented using table lookup
2 function [3:0] Sbox1;
3   input [5:0] in;
4   case(in)
5   6'h00:Sbox1=4'he;6'h01:Sbox1=4'h4;6'h02:Sbox1=4'hd;
```

```
 6    6'h03:Sbox1=4'h1;6'h04:Sbox1=4'h2;6'h05:Sbox1=4'hf;
 7    6'h06:Sbox1=4'hb;6'h07:Sbox1=4'h8;6'h08:Sbox1=4'h3;
 8    6'h09:Sbox1=4'ha;6'h0a:Sbox1=4'h6;6'h0b:Sbox1=4'hc;
 9    6'h0c:Sbox1=4'h5;6'h0d:Sbox1=4'h9;6'h0e:Sbox1=4'h0;
10    6'h0f:Sbox1=4'h7;6'h10:Sbox1=4'h0;6'h11:Sbox1=4'hf;
11    6'h12:Sbox1=4'h7;6'h13:Sbox1=4'h4;6'h14:Sbox1=4'he;
12    6'h15:Sbox1=4'h2;6'h16:Sbox1=4'hd;6'h17:Sbox1=4'h1;
13    6'h18:Sbox1=4'ha;6'h19:Sbox1=4'h6;6'h1a:Sbox1=4'hc;
14    6'h1b:Sbox1=4'hb;6'h1c:Sbox1=4'h9;6'h1d:Sbox1=4'h5;
15    6'h1e:Sbox1=4'h3;6'h1f:Sbox1=4'h8;6'h20:Sbox1=4'h4;
16    6'h21:Sbox1=4'h1;6'h22:Sbox1=4'he;6'h23:Sbox1=4'h8;
17    6'h24:Sbox1=4'hd;6'h25:Sbox1=4'h6;6'h26:Sbox1=4'h2;
18    6'h27:Sbox1=4'hb;6'h28:Sbox1=4'hf;6'h29:Sbox1=4'hc;
19    6'h2a:Sbox1=4'h9;6'h2b:Sbox1=4'h7;6'h2c:Sbox1=4'h3;
20    6'h2d:Sbox1=4'ha;6'h2e:Sbox1=4'h5;6'h2f:Sbox1=4'h0;
21    6'h30:Sbox1=4'hf;6'h31:Sbox1=4'hc;6'h32:Sbox1=4'h8;
22    6'h33:Sbox1=4'h2;6'h34:Sbox1=4'h4;6'h35:Sbox1=4'h9;
23    6'h36:Sbox1=4'h1;6'h37:Sbox1=4'h7;6'h38:Sbox1=4'h5;
24    6'h39:Sbox1=4'hb;6'h3a:Sbox1=4'h3;6'h3b:Sbox1=4'he;
25    6'h3c:Sbox1=4'ha;6'h3d:Sbox1=4'h0;6'h3e:Sbox1=4'h6;
26    6'h3f:Sbox1=4'hd;default:Sbox1=4'he;
27    endcase
28 endfunction
```

3.3.4 PERMUTATION

The 32-bit input is permuted as that shown in Table 3.11. The locations in the table from left to right, and from top to bottom, represent those from the 31st bit, i.e., MSB, of the output to its 0th bit, i.e., LSB. The number in Table 3.11 represents the bit position of input. For example, the first position in the upper left corner is the 31st bit of the output, which corresponds to the 16th bit of the input.

Table 3.11: Permutation.

16	25	12	11	3	20	4	15
31	17	9	6	27	14	1	22
30	24	8	18	0	5	29	23
13	19	2	26	10	21	28	7

The RTL code of permutation is written below, where in and out signals are 32-bit input and output, respectively. The permutation is implemented using rewiring without any logic gates.

```
1 // Permutation
2 wire [31:0] in;
3 wire [31:0] out;
4 assign out={in[16], in[25], in[12], in[11], in[3], in[20],
5            in[4], in[15],
6            in[31], in[17], in[9], in[6], in[27], in[14],
7            in[1], in[22],
8            in[30], in[24], in[8], in[18], in[0], in[5],
9            in[29], in[23],
10           in[13], in[19], in[2], in[26], in[10], in[21],
11           in[28], in[7]};
```

3.4 FINAL PERMUTATION

After 16 rounds of calculations, before outputting the result, it needs to be rearranged through the final permutation as that shown in Table 3.12. The locations in the table from left to right, and from top to bottom, represent those from the 63rd bit, i.e., MSB, of the output to its 0th bit, i.e., LSB. The number in Table 3.12 represents the bit position of input. For example, the first position in the upper left corner is the 63rd bit of the output, which corresponds to the 24th bit of the input.

Table 3.12: Final permutation.

24	56	16	48	8	40	0	32
25	57	17	49	9	41	1	33
26	58	18	50	10	42	2	34
27	59	19	51	11	43	3	35
28	60	20	52	12	44	4	36
29	61	21	53	13	45	5	37
30	62	22	54	14	46	6	38
31	63	23	55	15	47	7	39

The RTL code of final permutation is written below, where in and out signals are 64-bit input and output, respectively. The final permutation is implemented using rewiring without any logic gates.

```
1 // Final permutation
2 wire [63:0] in;
3 wire [63:0] out;
4 assign out={in[24], in[56], in[16], in[48], in[8], in[40],
5               in[0], in[32],
6               in[25], in[57], in[17], in[49], in[9], in[41],
7               in[1], in[33],
8               in[26], in[58], in[18], in[50], in[10], in[42],
9               in[2], in[34],
10              in[27], in[59], in[19], in[51], in[11], in[43],
11              in[3], in[35],
12              in[28], in[60], in[20], in[52], in[12], in[44],
13              in[4], in[36],
14              in[29], in[61], in[21], in[53], in[13], in[45],
15              in[5], in[37],
16              in[30], in[62], in[22], in[54], in[14], in[46],
17              in[6], in[38],
18              in[31], in[63], in[23], in[55], in[15], in[47],
19              in[7], in[39]};
```

3.5 SUBKEY GENERATION

The subkey generation process in DES plays a critical role in its encryption mechanism. Starting with a 64-bit key provided by the user, the algorithm reduces it to 56 bits by removing eight parity bits. This 56-bit key undergoes an initial permutation, known as permuted choice 1 (PC-1), which rearranges the key and splits it into two 28-bit halves. During each of the 16 encryption rounds, these halves are shifted left by 1 or 2 positions, depending on the round. After the shifts, a second permutation called permutation choice 2 (PC-2) reduces the 56-bit combined key to a 48-bit subkey, tailored for that specific round. This iterative process ensures that all 16 rounds operate with distinct subkeys, enhancing the algorithm's security by introducing variability and preventing straightforward attacks. The careful design of subkey generation is key to DES's effectiveness in maintaining cryptographic strength.

Specifically, the subkey generation is presented in Figure 3.3. The PC-1 selects 56 bits from the 64-bit initial key and then rearrange 56-bit output into two half keys with 28 bits each. In the next 16 rounds, the two half keys are left-rotated by one or two bits depending on the round number. Then, the two half-keys that have been left-rotated are used to generate subkeys through PC-2. As these functions closely resemble those of the initial permutation, F block, and final permutation, their corresponding RTL codes are not included in this section.

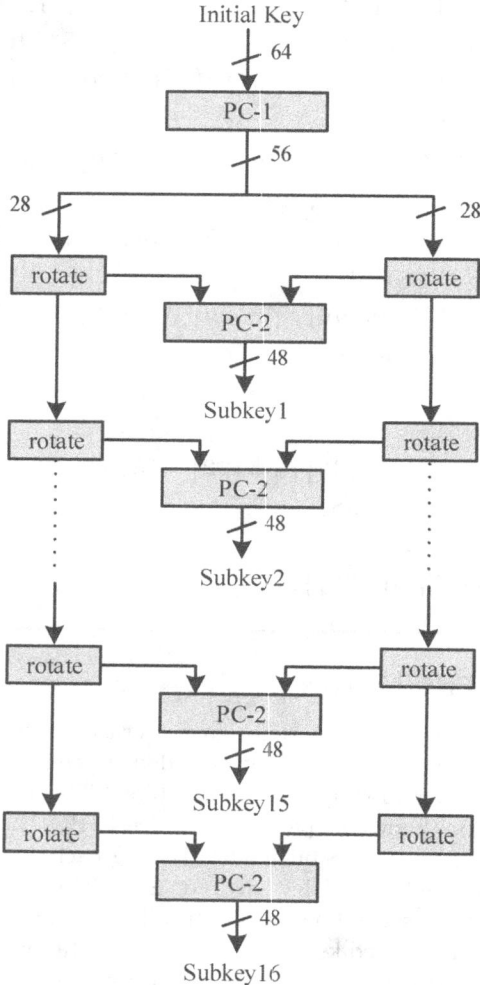

Figure 3.3: Flow chart of subkey generation.

3.5.1 PERMUTED CHOICE 1

The 64-bit input is permuted as that shown in Table 3.13. The locations in the table from left to right, and from top to bottom, represent those from the 55th bit, i.e., MSB, of the output to its 0th bit, i.e., LSB. The number in

Table 3.13 represents the bit position of input. For example, the first position in the upper left corner is the 55th bit of the output, which corresponds to the 7th bit of the input.

Table 3.13: Permuted choice 1.

7	15	23	31	39	47	55
63	6	14	22	30	38	46
54	62	5	13	21	29	37
45	53	61	4	12	20	28
1	9	17	25	33	41	49
57	2	10	18	26	34	42
50	58	3	11	19	27	35
43	51	59	36	44	52	60

3.5.2 ROTATE

In each round, two half keys need to be left-rotated according to Table 3.14, where offset represents the bit number of left rotation.

Table 3.14: Offset of left rotation.

Round number	1	2	3	4	5	6	7	8	9	10	11	12	13	14	15	16
Offset	1	1	2	2	2	2	2	2	1	2	2	2	2	2	2	1

3.5.3 PERMUTED CHOICE 2

The 56-bit input is permuted as that shown in Table 3.15. The locations in the table from left to right, and from top to bottom, represent those from the 47th bit, i.e., MSB, of the output to its 0th bit, i.e., LSB. The number in Table 3.15 represents the bit position of input. For example, the first position in the upper left corner is the 47th bit of the output, which corresponds to the 42nd bit of the input.

Table 3.15: Permuted choice 2.

42	39	45	32	55	51
53	28	41	50	35	46
33	37	44	52	30	48
40	49	29	36	43	54
15	4	25	19	9	1
26	16	5	11	23	8
12	7	17	0	22	3
10	14	6	20	27	24

3.5.4 FINAL SUBKEYS

Based on PC-1, rotation, and PC-2 of each subkeys, the final 16 subkeys can be directly derived from the initial key in Tables 3.16–3.31. The locations in the tables from left to right, and from top to bottom, represent those from the 47th bit, i.e., MSB, of the output to its 0th bit, i.e., LSB. The numbers in tables represent the bit position of input initial key. For example, the first position in the upper left corner is the 47th bit of the output, which corresponds to the 54th bit of the initial key in Table 3.16.

Table 3.16: Subkey 1.

54	13	30	4	15	47	31	7
62	55	45	22	61	29	38	39
20	6	5	63	28	37	46	23
42	36	25	10	27	60	17	34
59	11	41	35	3	43	26	1
49	44	19	50	51	2	9	33

Table 3.17: Subkey 2.

62	21	38	12	23	55	39	15
5	63	53	30	4	37	46	47
28	14	13	6	7	45	54	31
50	44	33	18	35	1	25	42
36	19	49	43	11	51	34	9
57	52	27	58	59	10	17	41

Table 3.18: Subkey 3.

13	37	54	28	39	6	55	31
21	14	4	46	20	53	62	63
15	30	29	22	23	61	5	47
3	60	49	34	51	17	41	58
52	35	2	59	27	36	50	25
10	1	43	11	44	26	33	57

Table 3.19: Subkey 4.

29	53	5	15	55	22	6	47
37	30	20	62	7	4	13	14
31	46	45	38	39	12	21	63
19	9	2	50	36	33	57	11
1	51	18	44	43	52	3	41
26	17	59	27	60	42	49	10

Table 3.20: Subkey 5.

45	4	21	31	6	38	22	63
53	46	7	13	23	20	29	30
47	62	61	54	55	28	37	14
35	25	18	3	52	49	10	27
17	36	34	60	59	1	19	57
42	33	44	43	9	58	2	26

Table 3.21: Subkey 6.

61	20	37	47	22	54	38	14
4	62	23	29	39	7	45	46
63	13	12	5	6	15	53	30
51	41	34	19	1	2	26	43
33	52	50	9	44	17	35	10
58	49	60	59	25	11	18	42

Table 3.22: Subkey 7.

12	7	53	63	38	5	54	30
20	13	39	45	55	23	61	62
14	29	28	21	22	31	4	46
36	57	50	35	17	18	42	59
49	1	3	25	60	33	51	26
11	2	9	44	41	27	34	58

Table 3.23: Subkey 8.

28	23	4	14	54	21	5	46
7	29	55	61	6	39	12	13
30	45	15	37	38	47	20	62
52	10	3	51	33	34	58	44
2	17	19	41	9	49	36	42
27	18	25	60	57	43	50	11

Table 3.24: Subkey 9.

7	31	12	22	62	29	13	54
15	37	63	4	14	47	20	21
38	53	23	45	46	55	28	5
60	18	11	59	41	42	3	52
10	25	27	49	17	57	44	50
35	26	33	1	2	51	58	19

Table 3.25: Subkey 10.

23	47	28	38	13	45	29	5
31	53	14	20	30	63	7	37
54	4	39	61	62	6	15	21
9	34	27	44	57	58	19	1
26	41	43	2	33	10	60	3
51	42	49	17	18	36	11	35

Table 3.26: Subkey 11.

39	63	15	54	29	61	45	21
47	4	30	7	46	14	23	53
5	20	55	12	13	22	31	37
25	50	43	60	10	11	35	17
42	57	59	18	49	26	9	19
36	58	2	33	34	52	27	51

Table 3.27: Subkey 12.

55	14	31	5	45	12	61	37
63	20	46	23	62	30	39	4
21	7	6	28	29	38	47	53
41	3	59	9	26	27	51	33
58	10	44	34	2	42	25	35
52	11	18	49	50	1	43	36

Table 3.28: Subkey 13.

6	30	47	21	61	28	12	53
14	7	62	39	13	46	55	20
37	23	22	15	45	54	63	4
57	19	44	25	42	43	36	49
11	26	60	50	18	58	41	51
1	27	34	2	3	17	59	52

Table 3.29: Subkey 14.

22	46	63	37	12	15	28	4
30	23	13	55	29	62	6	7
53	39	38	31	61	5	14	20
10	35	60	41	58	59	52	2
27	42	9	3	34	11	57	36
17	43	50	18	19	33	44	1

Table 3.30: Subkey 15.

38	62	14	53	28	31	15	20
46	39	29	6	45	13	22	23
4	55	54	47	12	21	30	7
26	51	9	57	11	44	1	18
43	58	25	19	50	27	10	52
33	59	3	34	35	49	60	17

Table 3.31: Subkey 16.

46	5	22	61	7	39	23	28
54	47	37	14	53	21	30	31
12	63	62	55	20	29	38	15
34	59	17	2	19	52	9	26
51	3	33	27	58	35	18	60
41	36	11	42	43	57	1	25

3.6 UNFOLDED AND SUB-PIPELINED DESIGN OF DES ENCRYPTION

This section emphasizes the high-throughput design of the DES encryption circuit, leveraging unfolded and sub-pipelined design techniques. Since DES decryption closely resembles encryption, only the encryption design is presented in this section. At the beginning, to obtain one result in a clock cycle, the 16 rounds of DES are unfolded, as presented in Figure 3.4.

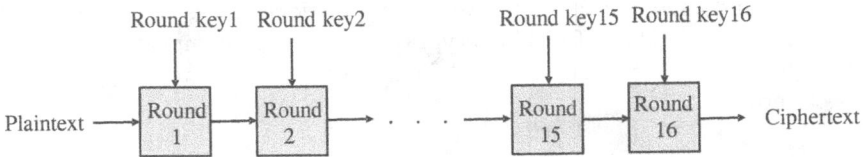

Figure 3.4: Overall unfolded DES encryption circuit.

Next, we adopt the sub-pipeline technique to increase the clock frequency of the unfolded design. Based on the RTL codes in the previous section, a pure combinational circuit of DES circuit can be simply obtained. However, to increase the clock frequency and throughput, pipeline technique is usually adopted. Making path delays balanced is the key point of pipelined circuits. We will treat the path delays of a 2-to-1 multiplexer and XOR as roughly the same. It can be observed that the S-box contains four 64-to-1 multiplexers. Besides, a 64-to-1 multiplexer (in Figure 3.5(a)) corresponds to 6-stage 2-to-1 multiplexers (in Figure 3.5(b)), where the dashed line represents the locations registers are inserted, the stage 1 contains 32 2-to-1 multiplexers in parallel, stage 2 contains 16 2-to-1 multiplexers in parallel, and so on. Consequently, the path delays of the 6-stage pipelined S-box are balanced with only one 2-to-1 multiplexer. Extra $32 + 16 + \ldots + 1 = 63$ pipeline registers are needed for single-bit output of S-box.

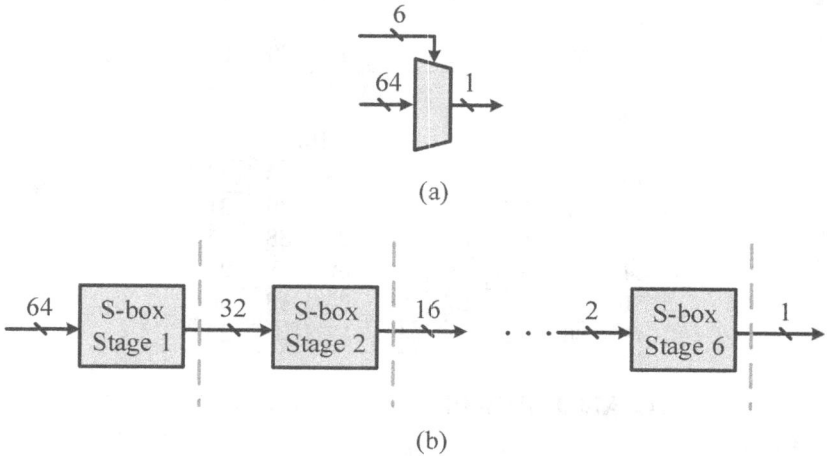

(a)

(b)

Figure 3.5: Single-bit output of S-box implemented using (a) one 64-to-1 multiplexer, and (b) 6-stage 2-to-1 multiplexers.

The expansion and permutation of F block have no logic gates in them, while the subkey mixing has a path delay of one XOR gate. Additionally, the initial and final permutations also have no logic gates in them. From above, the round circuit of DES encryption requires eight pipeline stages, as displayed in Figure 3.6, where E and P denote the expansion and permutation, respectively.

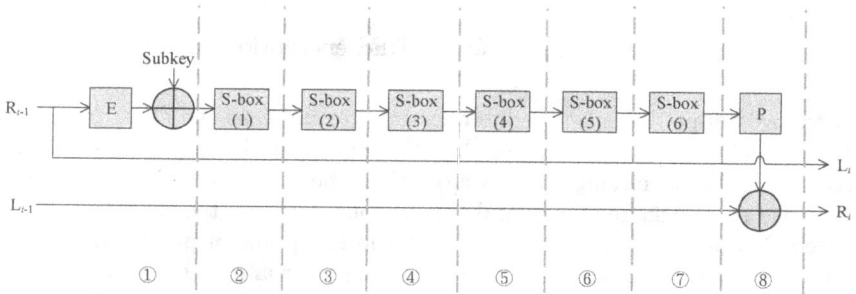

Figure 3.6: Pipelined round function of DES.

3.7 TRIPLE DES

With the advancement of technology, the key length of DES was too short to be easily cracked. Therefore, the 3DES encryption algorithm was invented to avoid easy cracking by increasing the key length. 3DES, introduced in the late 1970s, is also a symmetric key block cipher designed to enhance the security of the original DES.

3DES strengthens DES by applying the encryption process three times to each data block. Specifically, it is a concatenation of three consecutive DES algorithms, i.e., DES encryption-DES decryption-DES encryption, which use three different keys, as displayed in Figure 3.7(a). The plaintext is encrypted using the first key (Key1). The resulting ciphertext is decrypted using a second key (Key2). The output is re-encrypted using a third key (Key3). This triple application of DES ensures a higher level of security. Depending on the implementation, 3DES can use three independent keys (168-bit key length) or two keys (112-bit key length, where Key1 and Key3 are the same). Nevertheless, its 64-bit block size is relatively small by today's standards, making it vulnerable to certain attacks, such as block collisions in large datasets.

On the contrary, the decryption process of 3DES is performed in the reverse sequence of its encryption process. Hence, 3DES decryption is a concatenation of DES decryption-DES encryption-DES decryption, and the keys used for decryption are in the opposite order of the keys used for encryption, as displayed in Figure 3.7(b).

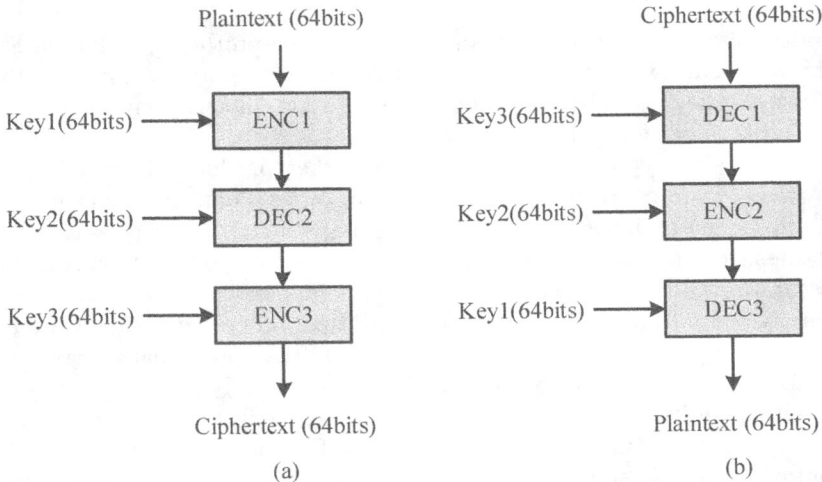

Figure 3.7: Triple DES (a) encryption, (b) decryption.

4 Secure Hash Algorithm

The secure hash algorithms (SHA) are a family of cryptographic hash functions designed to ensure data integrity and security. The SHA family consists of multiple versions tailored for different security needs. In 1993, SHA-0 was the original release but was quickly withdrawn due to vulnerabilities. SHA-1 followed in 1995, offering a 160-bit hash value, but is now considered insecure because of collision attacks. SHA-2 introduced several improved versions, which provide higher security and remain widely used. SHA-3 (formerly Keccak), standardized in 2015, utilizes a unique cryptographic structure distinct from its predecessors, offering enhanced resilience against emerging threats. Together, these variants play a vital role in modern cryptographic systems.

In 2001, SHA-2 was first ratified by National Institute of Standards and Technology (NIST) and became a FIPS standard. Nowadays, SHA-2 is also widely used in various trusted computing, internet of things (IoT) and blockchain technologies. The SHA-2 is composed of six algorithms, including SHA-224, SHA-256, SHA-384, SHA-512, SHA-512/224, and SHA-512/256. This section will focus on the design of SHA-256, where the number 256 designates the bit width of the hash value.

4.1 INTRODUCTION

SHA algorithms are integral to many cryptographic protocols, including SSL/TLS for secure web communications, blockchain technologies, and digital certificates. They are also used for verifying data integrity by generating unique hash values for files or messages.

SHA-256 is a cryptographic hash function that produces a fixed 256-bit hash value, regardless of the input size. It can process data of any length up to 2^{64} bits, denoted by the 64-bit length field appended to the message. The input message is padded to ensure its length is a multiple of 512 bits. A 64-bit representation of the original message length is appended. The padded message is divided into 512-bit blocks, which are then processed through several iterations using logical functions and constants. SHA-256 is characterized by its determinism, ensuring that the same input consistently produces the same hash value. Additionally, it exhibits the avalanche effect, where even a minor change in the input leads to a drastically different hash output. It is also computationally infeasible to reverse-engineer the input from the hash value.

Specifically, in SHA-256, a data block and a word have 512 bits and 32 bits, respectively. A 64-bit length field will be added at the end of original message. If the bit number of original message and length field is not a multiple of 512 bits, it requires that the data be padded to a full block if it is smaller than the block size, as that shown in Figure 4.1, where HC denotes the hash

DOI: 10.1201/9781003650553-4

computation and H^i denotes the hash value output of the HC of the i-th block. Each HC includes 64 iterative rounds. These involve bitwise operations, modular additions, and message mixing. In Figure 4.1, there are N blocks used to compute the final hash value, H^N.

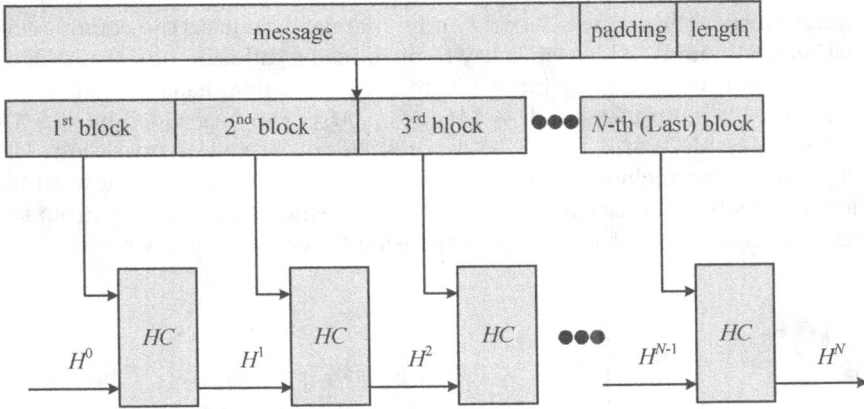

Figure 4.1: Structure of SHA-256 algorithm.

The HC for each block can be divided into two parts: message expansion and hash compression. After the hash computation of a block, we will get the i-th stage hash value $H^i = \{H_a^i, H_b^i, H_c^i, H_d^i, H_e^i, H_f^i, H_g^i, H_h^i\}$, initiated from the $(i-1)$-th stage hash value, H^{i-1}. The initial hash value, $H^0 = \{H_a^0, H_b^0, H_c^0, H_d^0, H_e^0, H_f^0, H_g^0, H_h^0\}$, is a constant and displayed in Table 4.1.

Table 4.1: Initial hash value.

Word	Value
H_a^0	$\{6a09e667\}_{16}$
H_b^0	$\{bb67ae85\}_{16}$
H_c^0	$\{3c6ef372\}_{16}$
H_d^0	$\{a54ff53a\}_{16}$
H_e^0	$\{510e527f\}_{16}$
H_f^0	$\{9b05688c\}_{16}$
H_g^0	$\{1f83d9ab\}_{16}$
H_h^0	$\{5be0cd19\}_{16}$

4.2 MESSAGE EXPANSION

The Message Expansion process in SHA-256 is a critical step that prepares the input message for hashing by generating a sequence of words used during the compression rounds. It ensures proper mixing of input data, enhancing the algorithm's resistance to cryptographic attacks. This expansion ensures that the message words interact non-linearly and dynamically during the compression function's 64 rounds. This step is key to introducing diffusion into the hashing process, ensuring that every input bit influences the final hash output.

The 512-bit input message $M = \{M_0, M_1,...,M_{15}\}$ can be divided into 16 32-bit words, $M_0, M_1,...,M_{15}$, where $\{\cdot\}$ denotes the concatenation operation. The hash compression includes 64 iterative rounds. Within each round, a word W_t, where $t = 0 \sim 63$ denotes the iterative round, is required and derived from the original message M by the message expansion function, which is written as

$$
W_t = \begin{cases} M_t, & \\ & 0 \leq t \leq 15, \\ \sigma_1(W_{t-2}) + W_{t-7} + \sigma_0(W_{t-15}) + W_{t-16}, & \\ & 16 \leq t \leq 63, \end{cases} \tag{4.1}
$$

where $+$ denotes the modular addition operation (modulo 2^{32}),

$$
\begin{aligned}
\sigma_0(x) &= ROTR^7(x) \oplus ROTR^{18}(x) \oplus SHR^3(x), \\
\sigma_1(x) &= ROTR^{17}(x) \oplus ROTR^{19}(x) \oplus SHR^{10}(x),
\end{aligned} \tag{4.2}
$$

$\oplus$ denotes the logic XOR operation, and $ROTR^y(x)$ and $SHR^y(x)$ right rotate and shift x by y bits, respectively. In the first 16 rounds, M_t is directly used as W_t, while, in remaining rounds, W_t is calculated by previous W_t's.

4.3 HASH COMPRESSION

The hash compression function is a core component of cryptographic hash algorithms like SHA-256. This stage iteratively processes message blocks and combines them with the current hash values to produce the final hash output. The hash compression function introduces non-linearity and diffusion into the hashing process, ensuring that even minor changes in the input produce significantly different hash outputs. It also ensures that the hash values depend on every part of the input, making reverse-engineering virtually impossible.

There are 64 iterative rounds in hash compression for each block, as presented in Figure 4.2. In each round t, $0 \leq t \leq 63$, eight variables, $a_t, b_t, c_t, d_t, e_t, f_t, g_t, h_t$, are calculated and updated using the iteration function

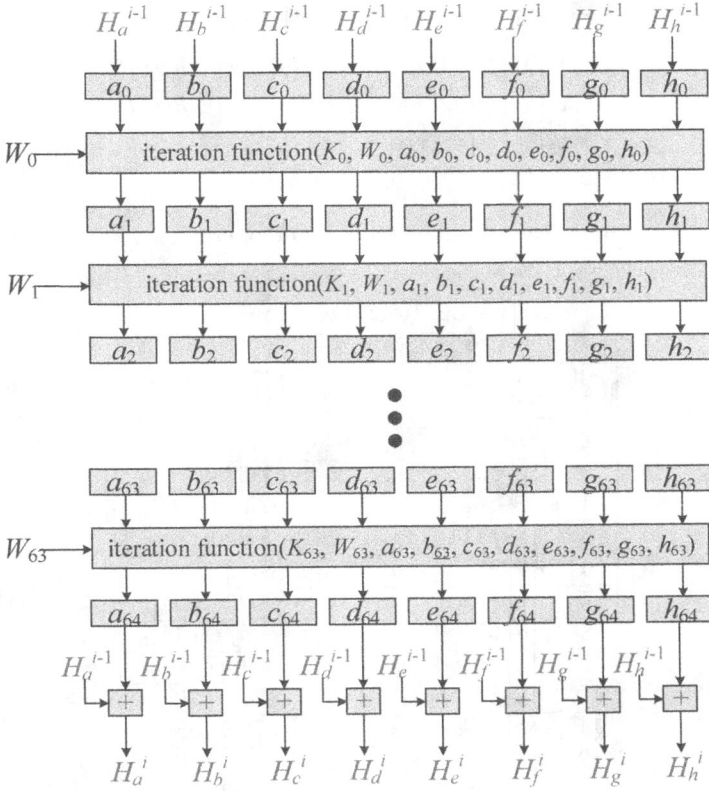

Figure 4.2: Hash computation.

by

$$\begin{cases}
a_{t+1} = T_{1,t} + T_{2,t}, \\
b_{t+1} = a_t, \\
c_{t+1} = b_t, \\
d_{t+1} = c_t, \\
e_{t+1} = d_t + T_{1,t}, \\
f_{t+1} = e_t, \\
g_{t+1} = f_t, \\
h_{t+1} = g_t, \\
T_{1,t} = \Sigma_1(e_t) + Ch(e_t, f_t, g_t) + K_t + W_t + h_t, \\
T_{2,t} = \Sigma_0(a_t) + Maj(a_t, b_t, c_t),
\end{cases} \qquad (4.3)$$

where K_t's are round constants displayed in Table 4.2,

$$
\begin{aligned}
\Sigma_0(x) &= ROTR^2(x) \oplus ROTR^{13}(x) \oplus ROTR^{22}(x), \\
\Sigma_1(x) &= ROTR^6(x) \oplus ROTR^{11}(x) \oplus ROTR^{25}(x), \\
Ch(x,y,z) &= (x \wedge y) \oplus (\bar{x} \wedge z), \\
Maj(x,y,z) &= (x \wedge y) \oplus (x \wedge z) \oplus (y \wedge z),
\end{aligned}
\tag{4.4}
$$

and $\wedge$ and $(\bar{\cdot})$ denote the logic AND and NOT operations, respectively.

Table 4.2: Round constants K_t.

t	K_t	t	K_t
0	$\{428a2f98\}_{16}$	32	$\{27b70a85\}_{16}$
1	$\{71374491\}_{16}$	33	$\{2e1b2138\}_{16}$
2	$\{b5c0fbcf\}_{16}$	34	$\{4d2c6dfc\}_{16}$
3	$\{e9b5dba5\}_{16}$	35	$\{53380d13\}_{16}$
4	$\{3956c25b\}_{16}$	36	$\{650a7354\}_{16}$
5	$\{59f111f1\}_{16}$	37	$\{766a0abb\}_{16}$
6	$\{923f82a4\}_{16}$	38	$\{81c2c92e\}_{16}$
7	$\{ab1c5ed5\}_{16}$	39	$\{92722c85\}_{16}$
8	$\{d807aa98\}_{16}$	40	$\{a2bfe8a1\}_{16}$
9	$\{12835b01\}_{16}$	41	$\{a81a664b\}_{16}$
10	$\{243185be\}_{16}$	42	$\{c24b8b70\}_{16}$
11	$\{550c7dc3\}_{16}$	43	$\{c76c51a3\}_{16}$
12	$\{72be5d74\}_{16}$	44	$\{d192e819\}_{16}$
13	$\{80deb1fe\}_{16}$	45	$\{d6990624\}_{16}$
14	$\{9bdc06a7\}_{16}$	46	$\{f40e3585\}_{16}$
15	$\{c19bf174\}_{16}$	47	$\{106aa070\}_{16}$
16	$\{e49b69c1\}_{16}$	48	$\{19a4c116\}_{16}$
17	$\{efbe4786\}_{16}$	49	$\{1e376c08\}_{16}$
18	$\{0fc19dc6\}_{16}$	50	$\{2748774c\}_{16}$
19	$\{240ca1cc\}_{16}$	51	$\{34b0bcb5\}_{16}$
20	$\{2de92c6f\}_{16}$	52	$\{391c0cb3\}_{16}$
21	$\{4a7484aa\}_{16}$	53	$\{4ed8aa4a\}_{16}$
22	$\{5cb0a9dc\}_{16}$	54	$\{5b9cca4f\}_{16}$
23	$\{76f988da\}_{16}$	55	$\{682e6ff3\}_{16}$
24	$\{983e5152\}_{16}$	56	$\{748f82ee\}_{16}$
25	$\{a831c66d\}_{16}$	57	$\{78a5636f\}_{16}$
26	$\{b00327c8\}_{16}$	58	$\{84c87814\}_{16}$
27	$\{bf597fc7\}_{16}$	59	$\{8cc70208\}_{16}$
28	$\{c6e00bf3\}_{16}$	60	$\{90befffa\}_{16}$
29	$\{d5a79147\}_{16}$	61	$\{a4506ceb\}_{16}$
30	$\{06ca6351\}_{16}$	62	$\{bef9a3f7\}_{16}$
31	$\{14292967\}_{16}$	63	$\{c67178f2\}_{16}$

During initialization, the eight variables $\{a_0, b_0, c_0, d_0, e_0, f_0, g_0, h_0\}$ of the i-th stage respectively load the $(i-1)$-th stage hash value $H^{i-1} = \{H_a^{i-1}, H_b^{i-1}, H_c^{i-1}, H_d^{i-1}, H_e^{i-1}, H_f^{i-1}, H_g^{i-1}, H_h^{i-1}\}$. After 64 iterative rounds, we get the variables $a_{64}, b_{64},..., h_{64}$. The hash value H^i of the i-th stage can be obtained by the final add step as

$$H^i = H^{i-1} + \{a_{64}, b_{64}, c_{64}, d_{64}, e_{64}, f_{64}, g_{64}, h_{64}\}. \tag{4.5}$$

4.4   RTL DESIGN

First, we introduce the RTL design of message expansion. By Equation 4.1, for $t = 16$, we have

$$W_{16} = \sigma_1(W_{14}) + W_9 + \sigma_0(W_1) + W_0. \tag{4.6}$$

Therefore, by Equation 4.2, W_{16} can be described using RTL by

```
1 // W16 implementation
2 wire [31:0] W16, W14, W9, W1, W0;
3 assign W16=sigma1(W14)+W9+sigma0(W1)+W0;
```

where overflow bits are naturally discarded as a result of the modular addition operation (modulo 2^{32}), and commonly used functions are listed below:

```
1 // sigma0 implementation
2 function [31:0] sigma0;
3    input [31:0] W;
4    sigma0=ROTR7(W)^ROTR18(W)^SHR3(W);
5 endfunction
6 // sigma1 implementation
7 function [31:0] sigma1;
8    input [31:0] W;
9    sigma1=ROTR17(W)^ROTR19(W)^SHR10(W);
10 endfunction
11 // ROTR7 implementation
12 function [31:0] ROTR7;
13    input [31:0] W;
14    ROTR7={W[6:0], W[31:7]};
15 endfunction
16 // ROTR18 implementation
```

```
17 function [31:0] ROTR18;
18   input [31:0] W;
19   ROTR18={W[17:0], W[31:18]};
20 endfunction
21 // SHR3 implementation
22 function [31:0] SHR3;
23   input [31:0] W;
24   SHR3=W>>3;
25 endfunction
26 // ROTR17 implementation
27 function [31:0] ROTR17;
28   input [31:0] W;
29   ROTR17={W[16:0], W[31:17]};
30 endfunction
31 // ROTR19 implementation
32 function [31:0] ROTR19;
33   input [31:0] W;
34   ROTR19={W[18:0], W[31:19]};
35 endfunction
36 // SHR10 implementation
37 function [31:0] SHR10;
38   input [31:0] W;
39   SHR10=W>>10;
40 endfunction
```

Next, we introduce the RTL design of hash compression. According to Equation 4.3, the iteration function is implemented using a module and can be written below.

```
1 // Iteration function
2 module iter_func(a_out, b_out, c_out, d_out, e_out, f_out,
3                  g_out, h_out, a_in, b_in, c_in, d_in,
4                  e_in, f_in, g_in, h_in, W, t);
5 output [31:0] a_out, b_out, c_out, d_out, e_out, f_out,
6                  g_out, h_out;
7 input [31:0] a_in, b_in, c_in, d_in, e_in, f_in,
```

```
8                g_in, h_in;
9  input  [31:0] W;
10 input  [5:0] t;
11 wire  [31:0] T1, T2;
12 reg  [31:0] K;
13 assign  a_out=T1+T2;
14 assign  b_out=a_in;
15 assign  c_out=b_in;
16 assign  d_out=c_in;
17 assign  e_out=d_in+T1;
18 assign  f_out=e_in;
19 assign  g_out=f_in;
20 assign  h_out=g_in;
21 assign  T1=Sigma1(e_in)+Ch(e_in,f_in,g_in)+K+W+h_in;
22 assign  T2=Sigma0(a_in)+Maj(a_in,b_in,c_in);
23 always  @(*)
24   case(t)
25   0: K=32'h428a2f98;  1: K=32'h71374491;
26   2: K=32'hb5c0fbcf;  3: K=32'he9b5dba5;
27   4: K=32'h3956c25b;  5: K=32'h59f111f1;
28   6: K=32'h923f82a4;  7: K=32'hab1c5ed5;
29   8: K=32'hd807aa98;  9: K=32'h12835b01;
30   10: K=32'h243185be;  11: K=32'h550c7dc3;
31   12: K=32'h72be5d74;  13: K=32'h80deb1fe;
32   14: K=32'h9bdc06a7;  15: K=32'hc19bf174;
33   16: K=32'he49b69c1;  17: K=32'hefbe4786;
34   18: K=32'h0fc19dc6;  19: K=32'h240ca1cc;
35   20: K=32'h2de92c6f;  21: K=32'h4a7484aa;
36   22: K=32'h5cb0a9dc;  23: K=32'h76f988da;
37   24: K=32'h983e5152;  25: K=32'ha831c66d;
38   26: K=32'hb00327c8;  27: K=32'hbf597fc7;
39   28: K=32'hc6e00bf3;  29: K=32'hd5a79147;
40   30: K=32'h06ca6351;  31: K=32'h14292967;
41   32: K=32'h27b70a85;  33: K=32'h2e1b2138;
42   34: K=32'h4d2c6dfc;  35: K=32'h53380d13;
```

```verilog
43    36:  K=32'h650a7354;  37:  K=32'h766a0abb;
44    38:  K=32'h81c2c92e;  39:  K=32'h92722c85;
45    40:  K=32'ha2bfe8a1;  41:  K=32'ha81a664b;
46    42:  K=32'hc24b8b70;  43:  K=32'hc76c51a3;
47    44:  K=32'hd192e819;  45:  K=32'hd6990624;
48    46:  K=32'hf40e3585;  47:  K=32'h106aa070;
49    48:  K=32'h19a4c116;  49:  K=32'h1e376c08;
50    50:  K=32'h2748774c;  51:  K=32'h34b0bcb5;
51    52:  K=32'h391c0cb3;  53:  K=32'h4ed8aa4a;
52    54:  K=32'h5b9cca4f;  55:  K=32'h682e6ff3;
53    56:  K=32'h748f82ee;  57:  K=32'h78a5636f;
54    58:  K=32'h84c87814;  59:  K=32'h8cc70208;
55    60:  K=32'h90befffa;  61:  K=32'ha4506ceb;
56    62:  K=32'hbef9a3f7;  63:  K=32'hc67178f2;
57    endcase
58  function [31:0] Ch;
59    input [31:0] x, y, z;
60    Ch=(x&y)^(~x&z);
61  endfunction
62  function [31:0] Maj;
63    input [31:0] x, y, z;
64    Maj=(x&y)^(x&z)^(y^z);
65  endfunction
66  function [31:0] Sigma0;
67    input [31:0] x;
68    Sigma0={x[1:0], x[31:2]}^{x[12:0], x[31:13]}^
69          {x[21:0], x[31:22]};
70  endfunction
71  function [31:0] Sigma1;
72    input [31:0] x;
73    Sigma1={x[5:0], x[31:6]}^{x[10:0], x[31:11]}^
74          {x[24:0], x[31:25]};
75  endfunction
76  endmodule
```

4.5 PIPELINED SHA-256 CORE

The calculation in an iterative round can be divided into two parts, the message expansion and hash compression, which are called expander and compressor in the digital blocks, respectively.

4.5.1 PIPELINED COMPRESSOR

We adopt 2-stage pipeline for each iterative round, i.e., pre-computation and post-computation, in Figure 4.3.

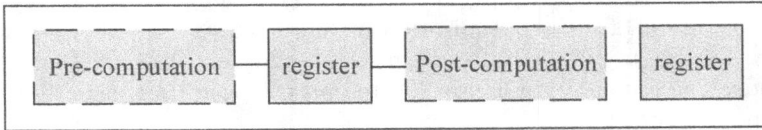

Figure 4.3: Two-stage pipeline of one iteration.

Intuitively, the 2-stage pipelined architecture is shown in Figure 4.4, where

$$\delta_t = K_t + W_t + h_t \tag{4.7}$$

and

$$P_t = \Sigma_1(e_t) + Ch(e_t, f_t, g_t). \tag{4.8}$$

As displayed, Figure 4.4 exhibits a critical path of two 32-bit adders, which is marked by the dot-dashed line. Notice that other non-critical paths are neglected in Figure 4.4.

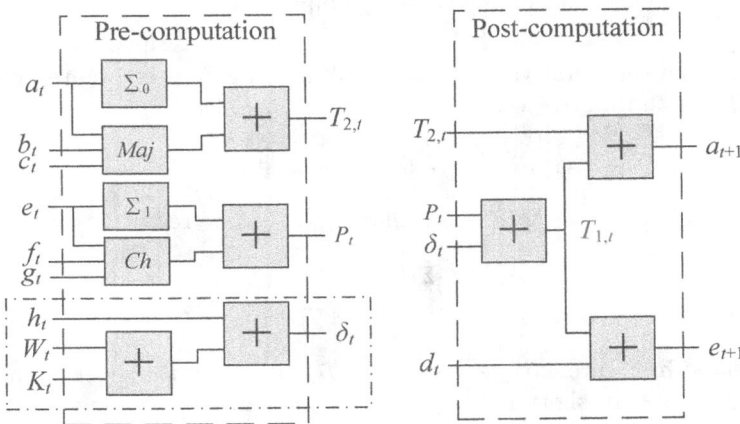

Figure 4.4: Original two-stage pipelined compressor.

Second, since $h_t = g_{t-1}$, δ_t can be rewritten as

$$\delta_t = K_t + W_t + g_{t-1}. \tag{4.9}$$

Therefore, $T_{1,t}$ can be expressed as

$$T_{1,t} \;=\; \Sigma_1(e_t) + Ch(e_t, f_t, g_t) + \delta_t. \tag{4.10}$$

Since W_t can be obtained in advance and K_t is a constant, δ_t can be moved from the pre-computation stage of the current iteration to the post-computation stage of the previous iteration. The improved architecture is shown in Figure 4.5. The optimization includes the use of carry-save adder (CSA), which is a good idea to optimize the addition of (more than) three operands. The critical path is now located on the path from e_t to $T_{1,t}$ in the first pipelined stage.

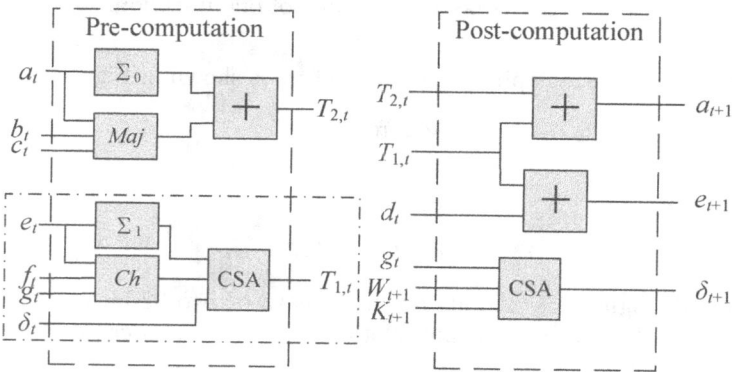

Figure 4.5: Improved 2-stage pipelined compressor.

Third, from the iterative Equation (4.3), e_t, f_t, and g_t can be represented by the $(t-1)$-th iterative variables:

$$e_t = d_{t-1} + T_{1,t-1}, \;\; f_t = e_{t-1}, \;\; g_t = f_{t-1}. \tag{4.11}$$

Therefore, the functions $\Sigma_1(e_t)$ and $Ch(e_t, f_t, g_t)$ can be rewritten as

$$\begin{aligned}
\Sigma_1(e_t) &= \Sigma_1(d_{t-1} + T_{1,t-1}), \\
Ch(e_t, f_t, g_t) &= Ch(d_{t-1} + T_{1,t-1}, e_{t-1}, f_{t-1}).
\end{aligned} \tag{4.12}$$

As presented in Figure 4.5, the path from $T_{1,t}$ to e_{t+1} in the second pipelined stage is a relatively short path. Therefore, we can pre-compute $\Sigma_1(e_t)$ and $Ch(e_t, f_t, g_t)$ of the first pipelined stage of the current iteration in the second pipelined stage of the previous iteration. As displayed in Figure 4.6, the critical paths of the two pipelined stages are almost balanced now.

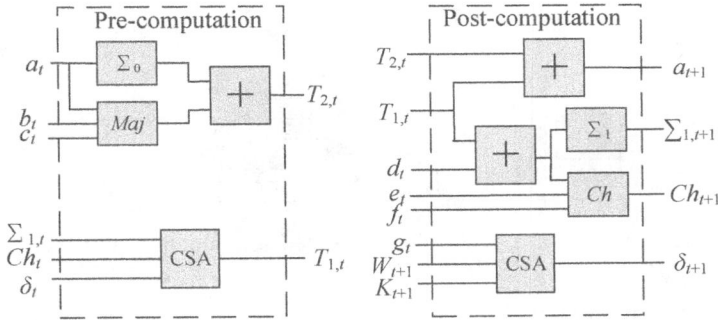

Figure 4.6: Delay-balanced compressor.

Fourth, as shown in Figure 4.6, the critical paths of the two pipeline stages are one 32-bit adder plus two or three logic gates. However, the path delay of the combinational logic function *Maj* is two logic XORs plus one logic AND. Compared with other logic gates, such as two-input AND or NOT gates, the XOR gate has a longer delay and will most likely cause the critical path. Consequently, we move the addition of the outputs of $\Sigma_0(a_t)$ and $Maj(a_t, b_t, c_t)$ from the first pipeline stage to the second pipeline stage, and then replace the addition of three operands by the CSA, as the final delay-balanced compressor shown in Figure 4.7. The critical path contains three logic gates (1XOR+1AND+1OR) and a 32-bit adder.

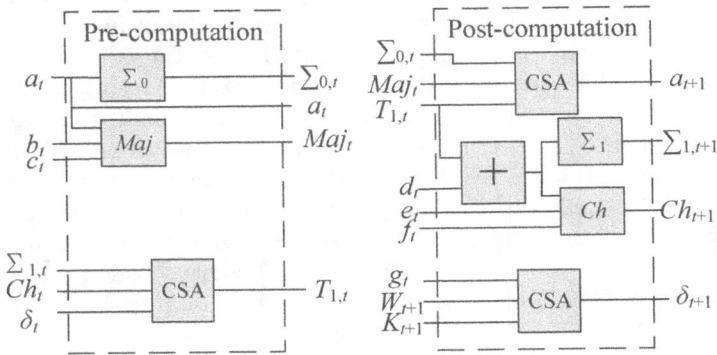

Figure 4.7: Final delay-balanced compressor.

4.5.2 PIPELINED EXPANDER

To work with the compressor, the expander in our work should also be 2-stage pipelined. The proposed expander is presented in Figure 4.8. It can be seen that its critical path is the same as that of the compressor.

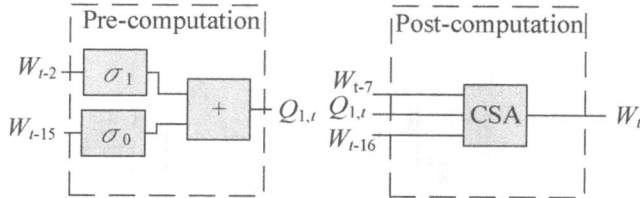

Figure 4.8: Delay-balanced expander.

4.6 BITCOIN MINING

Bitcoin is a decentralized digital currency. It operates on blockchain technology, a distributed public ledger that records all transactions and is maintained by nodes across the globe. Bitcoin operates without a central authority, such as a government or financial institution. Transactions are conducted directly between users, eliminating intermediaries. Bitcoin's total supply is capped at 21 million coins, making it a scarce asset and resistant to inflation. All transactions are recorded on the blockchain, ensuring transparency and immutability. Cryptographic techniques provide secure transaction processing. Hence, users can transact without revealing personal identities, although the transaction records are traceable.

In 2008, Satoshi Nakamoto proposed white paper of Bitcoin describing the Bitcoin protocol and how the blockchain works. Bitcoin uses the proof-of-work (PoW) technology as its decentralized consensus mechanism. Miners get valid PoW by constantly changing the nonce, a field of the input block header, and computing double SHA-256 for the block header until a valid nonce, which can create a hashing output smaller than the target value, has been found. The process of finding a valid nonce is called Bitcoin mining. In the worst case, a huge number of block headers with different nonces up to 2^{32}, needs to be processed by the double SHA-256. Compared to traditional applications of SHA-256 which requires to compute SHA-256 once, computational demand in Bitcoin mining has radically increased. Therefore, implementing a high efficient double SHA-256 engine has become an essential issue.

The double SHA-256 of the Bitcoin mining is shown in Figure 4.9. The input of the double SHA-256 is 640-bit block header, which is also the input of the first SHA-256 computation. A block header consists of the fields of 32-bit version, 256-bit previous block hash, 256-bit Merkle root, 32-bit time stamp, and 32-bit nonce. Each block of the header will be processed in tandem.

The flow chart of Bitcoin mining is presented in Figure 4.10. The final hash value is compared to the target value. If it is less than the target, it means that the mining is successful, and the result is output; otherwise, we need to adjust the random value (or nonce) and perform double SHA-256 again until the 2^{32} random numbers have been exhausted or the input block header changes. Miners usually initialize the random number to 32-bit zero,

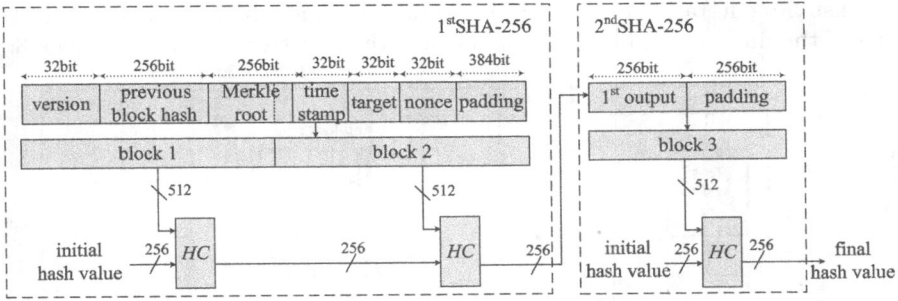

Figure 4.9: Double SHA-256 in Bitcoin mining.

and increase the random number by 1 each time as the input for the next operation.

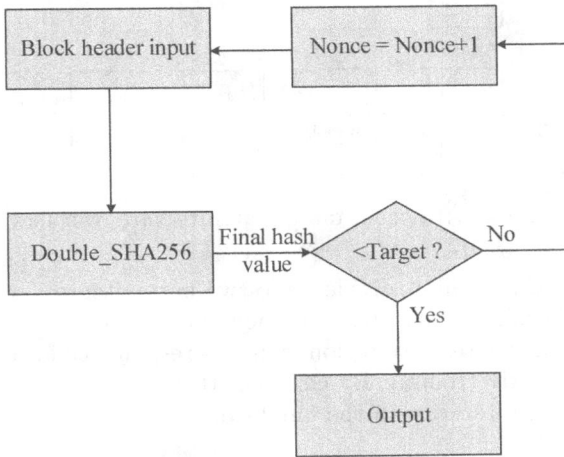

Figure 4.10: Flow chart of Bitcoin mining.

4.7 BITCOIN MINING ARCHITECTURE

As shown in Figure 4.9, the Bitcoin mining needs to compute double SHA-256 for the 640-bit input block header. The first and second SHA-256 computations contain two blocks and one block, respectively. To enhance the throughput and customize each iterative round, we adopt the Bitcoin mining circuit shown in Figure 4.11, where 120 iterative rounds are unfolded instead of folding whole 192 iterative rounds. The rationale is that the calculation of first 68 iterative rounds does not depend on the random nonce. Therefore, it can be computed once for all 2^{32} nonces. The calculation of the first iterative round of block 3 can be replaced by an addition due to the constant operand. Moreover, the last three iterative rounds can be ignored because the most significant 32 bits of the final hash value is available after the iterative round 60 of block 3.

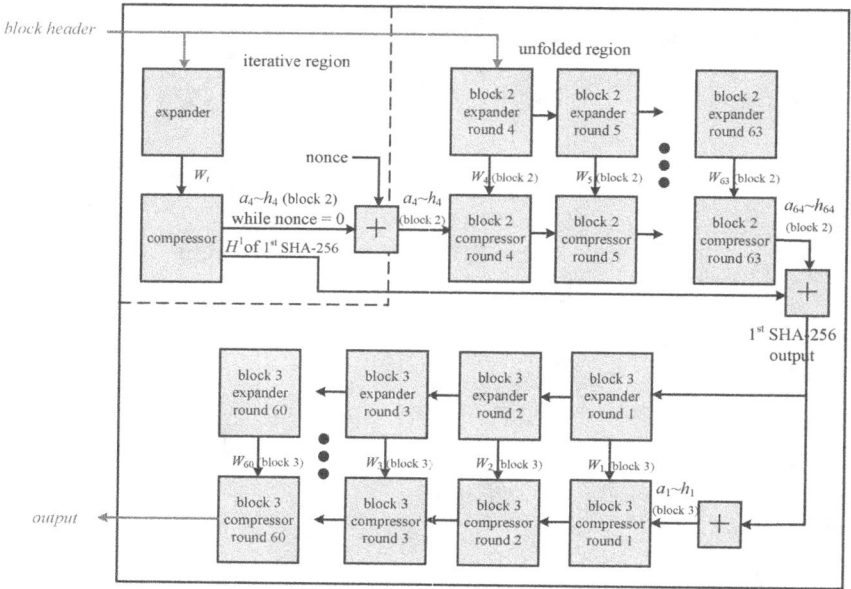

Figure 4.11: Bitcoin mining architecture overview.

The overall architecture is divided into two parts, iterative region and unfolded region. To enhance the area efficiency, there are only one expander and one compressor in the iterative region, which is responsible for the calculation of the first 68 iterative rounds. By contrast, there are one expander and one compressor for each iteration in the unfolded region.

4.7.1 THE ARCHITECTURE IN UNFOLDED REGION

The compressors and expanders in the unfolded region use the 2-stage pipelined SHA-256. Each compressor and expander are responsible for the calculation of a single iterative round.

The expanders in unfolded region can be optimized for specific iterative rounds. For example, the expanders to output $W_4 \sim W_{15}$ in block 2 and $W_1 \sim W_{15}$ in block 3 only require registers for pipeline, since there is no calculation to generate $W_0 \sim W_{15}$. Additionally, the padding consists of many constant zeros. Hence, there is no requirement to store these constants for pipeline with registers. Furthermore, if any one of the four operands in the message expansion function is zero, we can ignore the addition of the operand. The expander is customized with a simpler architecture in specific iterative round to save the chip area.

4.7.2 THE ARCHITECTURE IN ITERATIVE REGION

The compressor and expander in the iterative region are responsible for the calculation of the first 68 iterative rounds. The calculation of one iteration intuitively takes two clock cycles to complete with the multiplexer, as that shown in Figure 4.12(a). However, with the same combinational logics in the unfolded region, the extra control signal and multiplexer will cause the critical path to be located in the iterative region. Consequently, the original combinational logic of the pre-computation is divided into two parts, pre-computation1 and pre-computation2, as that shown in Figure 4.12(b). Likewise, the post-computation is divided into two parts, post-computation1 and post-computation2. As such, after shortening the critical path in the iterative region, the critical path must be located in the unfolded region.

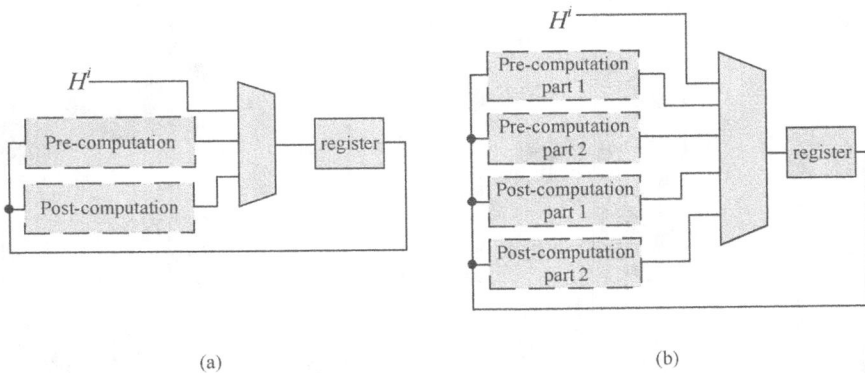

(a)   (b)

Figure 4.12: (a) Two clock cycles required for one iteration. (b) Four clock cycles required for one iteration.

Index

advanced encryption standard
  (AES), 7, 9, 10, 16–18, 20,
  22, 24, 26, 32, 33, 43, 47,
  58, 66, 70–72
add round key (AddRoundKey),
  17, 18, 20, 22–24, 27, 36,
  37, 44, 45, 54, 56, 57, 71
AES-128, 16
AES-192, 16
AES-256, 16
decryption, 23, 24, 27, 47, 57
decryption design, 57
encryption, 24, 26, 27, 44, 45,
  47, 57
encryption design, 45, 49, 57
Galois field, 17, 32, 33, 59, 62
inverse mix columns
  (InvMixColumns), 17, 24,
  26, 27, 41, 42, 57
inverse S-box, 21, 23, 24, 38, 57
inverse shift rows
  (InvShiftRows), 17, 24, 26,
  40, 57
inverse substitute bytes
  (InvSubBytes), 17, 20, 24,
  26, 38, 57, 58
key expansion, 18, 20, 22–24
mix columns (MixColumns), 17,
  18, 20–22, 26, 32–35, 44, 54,
  57, 71
round key, 17, 18, 20, 22–24, 36
RTL, 26, 29, 33–36, 42, 43, 45,
  49
S-box, 20, 21, 23, 24, 38, 54, 57,
  58
shift rows (ShiftRows), 17, 18,
  20, 21, 24, 26, 30, 31, 44,
  45, 54, 71
state, 17, 20–22, 24, 26, 29–31,
  34–37, 40, 42, 43, 56, 70
substitute bytes (SubBytes), 17,

18, 20, 21, 24, 26, 27, 29,
  44, 54, 57, 58, 71
  xtime, 32, 33
Bitcoin, 102
  mining, 102, 103
blockchain, 90, 102
carry-save adder (CSA), 100, 101
critical path, 47, 54, 58, 59, 62–65,
  99–101, 105
crypto engine, 3–8, 11, 68
cryptographic, 3–12, 14–16, 18,
  70–72, 81, 90, 92, 102
  algorithm, 7–9
  ciphertext, 4, 9, 17, 18, 20, 23,
    24, 45, 47, 54, 57, 66–68,
    72, 89
  hash, 3, 4, 10, 12, 14, 15, 90–92,
    95, 102, 104
  key, 4, 6, 8, 9, 11, 17, 18, 20,
    22–24, 44, 47, 49, 70–73, 76,
    81–84, 89
  key management, 4–7, 11
  plaintext, 4, 9, 17, 18, 23, 24, 29,
    44, 54, 57, 66–68, 72–74, 89
  private key, 10, 12–15
  protocol, 4–6, 8, 11, 12, 15, 16,
    90
  public key, 10, 12, 14, 70
  standard, 6, 8
cryptography, 66, 72
  asymmetric, 4, 7, 9, 10, 12
  block cipher, 10, 16, 17, 66, 68,
    89
  post-quantum cryptography, 8,
    70
  public-key cryptography, 14
  symmetric, 4, 7, 9, 10, 16, 70,
    72, 89
cyber threats, 1–3, 7, 11
  block collision attack, 89
  collision attack, 90

Denial-of-service (DoS) attacks, 2
Malware, 2
Man-in-the-middle (MitM) attacks, 2
Phishing attacks, 1
Quantum attack, 70
Ransomware, 1
recovery attacks, 72
cybersecurity, 1–3, 6–10, 12
authenticity, 2–5, 10–15, 66, 70
confidentiality, 3, 4, 8, 11, 15, 66
integrity, 1–5, 8, 11–13, 15, 70, 90
non-repudiation, 2, 4, 12, 14, 15
privacy, 11
data encryption standard (DES), 7, 9, 10, 16, 72–75, 81, 87, 89
decryption, 73, 89
decryption design, 87
encryption, 73, 81, 89
encryption design, 87, 88
expansion (E), 73, 75, 76, 88
F block, 73, 77, 82, 88
Feistel structure, 72, 73
final permutation, 72, 73, 80, 82, 88
initial permutation, 72–74, 82, 88
key scheduling, 73
permutation (P), 73, 80, 88
permuted choice 1 (PC-1), 81, 84
permuted choice 2 (PC-2), 81, 82, 84
RTL, 74, 76, 80, 82, 87
S-box, 73, 77, 78, 87, 88
subkey, 72, 73, 76, 81, 82, 84
subkey generation, 81
subkey mixing, 73, 76, 77, 88
digital signature algorithm (DSA), 2, 12–15
elliptic curve cryptography (ECC), 7, 10

Internet of things (IoT), 2, 3, 6, 8, 16, 90
mode of operation, 66
cipher-block chaining (CBC), 66
Galois/Counter mode (GCM), 70
pipeline, 16, 66, 87, 99, 101, 104
register, 44, 45, 47, 54, 56, 57, 88
stage, 88, 101
sub-pipeline, 54, 57, 87
Rijndael-256, 70, 71
Rivest-Shamir-Adleman (RSA), 7, 10, 14
secure hash algorithms (SHA), 90
SHA-0, 90
SHA-1, 90
SHA-2, 90
SHA-224, 90
SHA-3, 90
SHA-384, 90
SHA-512, 90
SHA-512/224, 90
SHA-512/256, 90
SHA-256, 13, 90, 92, 102–104
double SHA-256, 102, 103
hash compression, 91, 92, 96, 99
hash computation (HC), 90, 91
message expansion, 91, 92, 95, 99, 104
RTL, 95, 96
timing diagram, 47, 54
triple DES (3DES), 9, 10, 72, 89
unfold, 16, 47, 49, 66, 87, 104

For Product Safety Concerns and Information please contact our EU
representative GPSR@taylorandfrancis.com
Taylor & Francis Verlag GmbH, Kaufingerstraße 24, 80331 München, Germany

www.ingramcontent.com/pod-product-compliance
Lightning Source LLC
Chambersburg PA
CBHW052015230326
41598CB00078B/3487